Crown and People

THE YOUNG OXFORD HISTORY OF

BRITAIN & IRELAND

Crown and People

1500 ~ 1700

ROSEMARY KELLY

General Editor

PROFESSOR KENNETH O. MORGAN

OXFORD

UNIVERSITY PRESS

OXFORD
UNIVERSITY PRESS

Great Clarendon Street, Oxford OX2 6DP

Oxford University Press is a department of the University of Oxford.
It furthers the University's objective of excellence in research, scholarship,
and education by publishing worldwide in

Oxford New York

Athens Auckland Bangkok Bogotá Buenos Aires
Cape Town Chennai Dar es Salaam Delhi Florence Hong Kong Istanbul
Karachi Kolkata Kuala Lumpur Madrid Melbourne Mexico City Mumbai
Nairobi Paris São Paulo Shanghai Singapore Taipei Tokyo Toronto Warsaw

with associated companies in Berlin Ibadan

Oxford is a registered trade mark of Oxford University Press
in the UK and in certain other countries

Paperback ISBN 0–19–910830-7

1 3 5 7 9 10 8 6 4 2

Designed by Richard Morris, Stonesfield Design
Printed in China by Imago

CONTENTS

❖

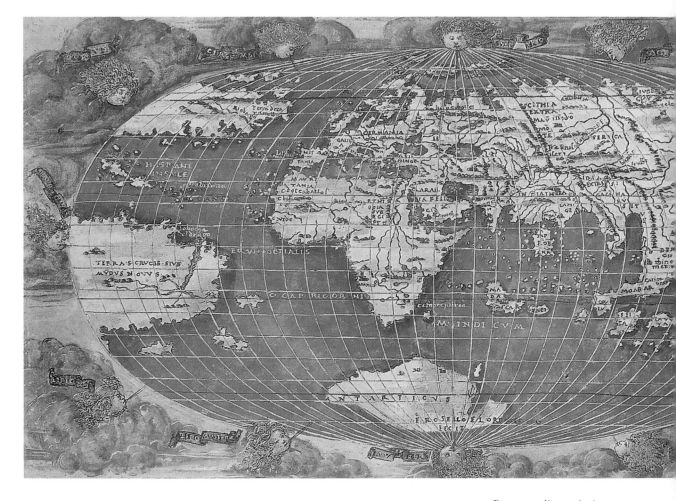

By 1500, discoveries in
learning and art were changing
the world of educated people in
Europe. These changes are now
called the Renaissance,
meaning rebirth. Horizons were
also widening. In the 1490s
the explorer Christopher
Columbus reached the coasts of

6

Chapter 1

Changing times

❖

*an unknown 'New World',
America, and Portuguese
ships found their way round
Southern Africa, and sailed
on to the riches of India and
the East. Soon map makers
like this one showed they knew
something of Africa, the East
and America.*

I never liked anything so much before. I find the climate both pleasant and
wholesome; and I have met with so much kindness and so much learning.

This is what the Dutch scholar, Erasmus, thought of England on his first
visit there in 1499 (although he later changed his mind about the
weather). At that time, Erasmus and other European scholars were re-
discovering the work of the writers, thinkers and scientists of ancient
Greece and Rome, which gave them exciting new ideas about the world
around them.

For centuries, scholars had studied Latin, the language of the Roman
Empire, which was still used by the Church and by governments for all
important matters. Scholars who were re-discovering the ideas of Greece
and Rome believed that the older civilization of Greece, which had
inspired the Romans, was the key to the understanding of human beings,
and opened the way to a new learning. They were called 'humanists' and
believed their studies would help to bring peace to the world, and
overcome poverty. Many humanists were religious men who wanted the
Church to give up worldly power and riches, and go back to the teaching
of Jesus in the Bible.

Erasmus became a close friend of the English lawyer and humanist
scholar, Thomas More, and visited his busy cultured household several
times. Other interesting visitors to More's household included the artist
Hans Holbein. In 1526 he arrived from his home town of Basel in
Switzerland, with a letter of introduction from Erasmus. More was
delighted with Holbein's brilliantly lifelike pictures of himself and his
family, and although he was worried about finding Holbein enough work,
he wrote back, 'Your painter, dearest Erasmus, is a wonderful artist'.

More was devoted to his family and, unusually for his time, believed
his three daughters should be as well educated as his son. When he was
away, he wrote home almost daily in Latin, and expected his children to
reply in Latin as well. He was deeply religious. When young he nearly

became a monk, but like many humanists, he also believed he should live in the world and try to change it for the better. This may have been why, in 1518, he became an important adviser to a magnificent, proud and powerful king.

A most accomplished prince

When Henry VIII (1509–1547) came to the throne, Thomas More joined a chorus of flattering praise for the eighteen-year-old king, declaring that 'sadness is at an end, and joy's before.' The athletic and well-educated young Henry impressed many people, including foreigners. The Venetian ambassador wrote in 1515:

> His Majesty is the handsomest potentate [ruler] I have ever set eyes on; above the usual height, with an extremely fine calf to his leg, his complexion very fair and bright, with auburn hair combed short and straight … He speaks French, English and Latin, and a little Italian, plays well on the lute and harpsichord, sings from book at sight, draws the bow with greater strength than any man in England, and jousts marvellously … he is in every respect a most accomplished prince.

Hans Holbein's sketch for a painting of Thomas More and his family in 1527, as they prepared for daily prayers at their house in Chelsea (which was then a village near London). More, wearing the official chain of a royal adviser, sits between his father and son. Books litter the floor. More's wife Alice, kneeling on the right, has a monkey nestling in her skirts, while through the doorway two clerks continue their work. More sent this drawing as a birthday present to Erasmus, who wrote: 'I should scarcely be able to see you better if I were with you.'

Henry the athlete, jousting before Queen Catherine in 1511, to celebrate the birth of their son. His marriage in 1509 to his dead brother Arthur's widow, the Spanish princess Catherine of Aragon, was popular, and began happily, but the baby boy died a month after he was born.

Henry himself was the centre of a magnificent court. By the end of his reign he owned fifty-five palaces, including Whitehall, Hampton Court and Greenwich, and he and the court moved from one to another as he chose. As in the past, the country was governed from wherever the king held court, but in these palaces the nerve centre of the royal household was no longer the great hall, as in a medieval castle. Beyond the hall, and protected by the royal guard, was the Presence Chamber, where the king held his councils and received important visitors. Beyond that was the Privy Chamber, where the king lived and worked privately; a modern historian has called it a grand royal version of a 'bedsit'.

Henry VIII's father, the shrewd, careful Henry VII, had kept an impressive court, but was a remote and distant man, working hard to keep his kingdom under control. Only a few chosen advisers and courtiers went into his Privy Chamber, where he spent long hours checking his accounts, writing dispatches and reading state papers.

The new king burst like a brilliant firework on to the old way of doing things. The honoured and chosen courtiers allowed into the Privy Chamber to attend to his personal needs were now his young jousting and hunting companions. When his mood changed, he would summon his favourite musicians and scholars. The king so enjoyed Thomas More's conversation that More had to try to make it less interesting so that Henry would allow him to go home to his family. The king liked to discuss,

astronomy, geometry, divinity [religion]… and sometimes … his worldly affairs… And other whiles would he in the night have him up into his leads [roof] there for to consider with him the… courses… of the stars and planets.

Scholars like Erasmus and artists like Holbein in England relied on patrons to provide them with a living. These might be the king or important men and women, such as Thomas More, who employed or befriended them in their households. Margaret Beaufort, the mother of Henry VII, gave money to colleges at both Oxford and Cambridge Universities, and also helped Caxton the printer (see page 12).

The new learning which these patrons so admired spread slowly at first, among scholars in London, the universities of Oxford and Cambridge, and the three Scots universities of St Andrews, Glasgow and Aberdeen. The invention of printing soon turned this trickle of new ideas and information into a flood (see page 12).

The confident richly dressed nobleman on the left of this picture was the French ambassador visiting the court of Henry VIII in 1533. While he was there, the ambassador ordered Holbein to paint this life-size picture of himself, and his friend, the serious-looking bishop on the right. The two men stand on each side of a table full of objects, so realistic you could almost pick them up, to show their interests in astronomy, mathematics, music and religion.

There is a clever puzzle in Holbein's picture. These two important and successful young men do not seem to notice the strange distorted object on the floor, yet they must have told Holbein to paint it there. From a viewpoint on the right-hand side of the picture, the object becomes a skull. It was an old idea to put a reminder of death in portraits, but Holbein paints it in an entirely new way.

Inkhorn, pen and hornbook

Some children had a better chance than others to go to school in the sixteenth century. In Scottish, Welsh and English towns, local businessmen or generous landowners founded free 'grammar schools' for local boys. Over 300 new schools were started in England alone in the sixteenth century. John Shakespeare was a glove maker in Stratford-on-Avon who never learnt to read. Although his business was doing badly, he managed to send his son William to the free grammar school in the town in 1571,

Young children learned to read from horn books, sometimes in 'petty [little] schools', but more often at home from their mothers. A horn book was a wooden board with a handle, protected by a sheet of transparent horn. It was a tough object, unlikely to break if a child dropped it or threw it around. It had letters and words on it, usually the alphabet and the Lord's Prayer, which children had to learn by heart.

and so set the boy on the path to becoming one of the world's most famous writers.

Girls seldom went to school. They might learn to read at home, but were mostly only taught the household skills they would need when they married. Only in a few rich and cultured households, such as Thomas More's, were girls as well educated as boys.

Country children from poor families might learn to read and write (often in schools held in the church porch) until they were about seven, and old enough to help keep the family going by working in the fields or at home. However some villages did have proper schools. In 1593 in Willingham in Cambridgeshire the villagers paid a £1 each (about a year's rent) to set up a school which was to last for 300 years.

Although many children never went to school, a growing number of people could read, and the increasing number of printed books meant that there was more for them to read. Going to school, even if it was often boring and sometimes painful, could give people the chance to go up in the world.

A crowded grammar school, with five classes in one room and at least one pupil getting a beating. The school day was long, often stretching from 7.00 a.m. to 5.00 p.m. The boys (there are no girls) studied Latin grammar, religion, some geography, arithmetic and music. Pupils had to provide their own books, candles and writing equipment. This would include a quill pen made from a trimmed feather with a sharpened point, a penknife to trim the point of the quill, an inkhorn and stopper, and a dust box (usually sand) used to dry the writing.

THE MIRACLE OF PRINTING

In about 1450, when books in Europe were rare, expensive and written by hand, Johann Gutenberg, a goldsmith in the German city of Mainz, set up the first European printing press. He used movable type, a method invented by the Chinese over 600 years earlier. Soon printing became quick and reasonably cheap.

The result was an explosion of printed books, which helped to increase the already growing numbers of people who could read – from scholars and royal ministers to tradespeople and craftsmen. News and ideas of all kinds spread more quickly. From the 1520s, as religious divisions split the Christian Church, individual religious beliefs were strengthened by printed Bibles which

A printing press illustrated in a book published in Germany in 1568. In the background two printers prepare each page by putting movable type into wooden frames. On the right, a worker uses pads to cover the type with ink before it goes into the press,

which is built like the wine and cider presses that had been in use in Europe for centuries. The press will force the paper hard on to the inked type. In front, the printed pages have been taken out of the press, and are stacked up ready to be bound into a book.

The printing workshops of the Plantin family in Antwerp were part of their home. They included the typefoundry, where the type was made, the workshop, type store, correctors' room, bookshop and office. Today, the house and workshops are preserved as a museum. This is the printing office, with type cases on one side and on the other a row of seventeenth and eighteenth century presses. At the end of the room are the two oldest presses in the world.

people could read in their own language, rather than in Latin. Rulers and churchmen in Europe soon realized that printing spread ideas which might threaten their power, so censorship – the control of printed books and pamplets – increased. In 1530 Henry VIII forbade his subjects to read 'pestiferous books, printed in other regions and sent into this realm'. In order to control books printed in England, Mary I set up the Stationers' Company in 1557; only its members were allowed to be printers.

Elizabeth I allowed printing presses to operate only in London, Oxford and Cambridge, and everything they printed had to be approved by her bishops. In 1579 a secret press published a pamphlet by John Stubbs, a lawyer, which condemned the queen's possible marriage to a French prince. Both Stubbs and his printer were publicly punished by having their right hands cut off.

In spite of strict rules, and occasional cruel punishments, it was always difficult to control printing. Presses were often quite small, and could be easily hidden or moved. Books were smuggled in from the flourishing printing houses of Europe. It was even more difficult to control the ideas and knowledge which people gained from reading. As the scientist and politician Francis Bacon wrote in 1597, 'Reading maketh a full man.'

One of the oldest presses used in the Plantin workshop. In the sixteenth and seventeenth centuries the Plantins were one of the most important printers in Europe.

Chapmen, or travelling pedlars, sold cheap ballads and newsheets as well as beads, ribbons and lace, in villages, towns and fairs. From the late 1500s they sold 'chapbooks', cheap little books costing a few pennies, so some villagers must have been able to read well enough to want to buy them. 'Merry books' were adventure stories, ghost stories, love stories and old favour-ites such as Jack and the Beanstalk and Red Riding Hood. 'Godly books' included Bible stories and advice on living a good life.

The trade mark of William Caxton, who set up the first English printing press at Westminster in 1476. Caxton was a rich merchant who learned his printing skills when trading in the Netherlands. His early bestsellers included Chaucer's Canterbury Tales and a book about chess.

Going up in the world

Four of the forty-two coats of arms, or family badges, set in the windows of Montacute House in Somerset. This great house was built in the 1590s by Sir Edward Phelips, a successful lawyer and Member of Parliament. As well as his own coat of arms, he included those of important people likely to visit his grand new house, friends at court and neighbouring landowners.

This picture of Lord Cobham and his family painted in 1567 shows them surrounded by evidence of their wealth and importance: clothes, family pets and expensive food on the table. The eldest son and heir, William, aged six, sits by his father. His two younger brothers still wear long skirts, as all small children in rich families did. The five-year-old twin girls and their four-year-old sister are just old enough to be dressed like miniature adults.

William Harrison, an Elizabethan clergyman who wrote a *Description of England* published in 1577, called the people at the top of society the 'First Sort':

> Of gentlemen the first and chief (next the King) be ... lords and noblemen, next unto them be knights ... and last of all they that be simply called gentlemen.

These families owned most of the land, but only numbered about two per cent of the population. Land meant wealth, so they were the ones with power. At court the most important of them were royal councillors, or those close to the monarch in the Privy Chamber. Many sat in Parliament. In their local area they owned the land and most of the houses where everyone else lived. They were the main employers, and as Justices of the Peace (or magistrates) they fixed wages, saw to the upkeep of roads and bridges, and enforced the law.

Clothes showed a person's place in society. Between 1519 and 1597 nineteen different laws tried to enforce what materials and colours people could wear, according to their rank. In 1553 no one other than an earl was supposed to wear cloth of gold and silver, furs, crimson, scarlet or blue velvet. Probably the few who could afford such luxuries bought them anyway, whatever their rank.

A gentleman's marriage was a business deal probably made by his parents when he was quite young while there was still plenty of choice of suitable partners. A new wife's dowry (the money and lands she brought

Hardwick Hall, built in the latest fashion and described as 'more glass than wall', was finished in 1597 when its owner Bess of Hardwick, was seventy-six. She was born the daughter of a simple Derbyshire gentleman, but by making four good marriages, she rose to be a great court lady. The initials ES on the towers proudly proclaim her rank: Elizabeth, Countess of Shrewsbury.

with her when she married) would, as in earlier times, be an important addition to his estates.

Ordinary villagers often did not marry until their late twenties, when they could afford to set up house. Rich or poor, the parents expected to make the choice for the young couple. We can only guess the story behind the will of a farmworker in Derbyshire who died in 1590. He left one cow and part of a bed to his daughter Ann, 'if she will forsake Robert Huit and be ruled by her mother'. There was little that was new in all this, but more people went up in the world during the sixteenth century.

Thomas Cromwell, the son of a Putney blacksmith, had a good education and the right patron to give him a job: Thomas Wolsey, the Lord Chancellor of England and the son of a butcher himself. Cromwell became Henry VIII's chief minister for eight years, and Henry made him Earl of Essex. Education, marriage, the right patron and hard work helped some people to join that powerful top two per cent of society, the 'First Sort'.

The 'great increase of people'

After the terrible plague, the Black Death, 150 years earlier, the number of people living in Britain had continued to decrease, but by 1500 this decline had halted. Between 1500 and 1600, the population of England alone probably doubled from 2.5 to 4.5 million. People at the time certainly noticed this change. In 1577 William Harrison in his *Description of England* wrote of ' a great increase of people'. These growing numbers altered the way in which people lived. An observer in 1549 wrote sadly,

> I have seen a cap for 14 pence, as good as I can get now for 18 pence... a pair of shoes cost me 12 pence now, that I have in my days [past] bought a better for six pence...

The rising price of essential goods, especially food, shocked sixteenth-century people, and was very hard on labourers, whose average pay was no more than five pence a day. Expensive wars and bad harvests also helped to push prices up at times, but the main cause was the simple fact that there were more people who needed these basic necessities, and not enough to go round. Things in short supply become expensive.

Some people did well out of high food prices especially those who owned or rented land which produced food. Many yeomen farmers prospered. These were farmers who often rented their land at a fixed sum. Since this did not go up many of them were better off. They sold their produce at good prices, and did not spend money on expensive luxuries in the way that 'the First Sort' did.

The increase in people often meant that there was not enough work, either on the land or in towns. Landowners and tradesmen no longer had to pay high wages to attract workers. Low wages and high prices hit poor families increasingly hard, and those without work often wandered desperately from place to place in search of it. Some probably turned to begging and stealing. Landowners and city officials certainly thought that this was so.

There was also often not enough land for the increasing population. In some areas changes in the way land was used made the problem worse. The wool and cloth trade was still England's main industry so there were good profits in sheep farming. Some landowners therefore, mainly in the midlands, continued to enclose land, fencing in fields to keep sheep, and sometimes taking for themselves the open fields where the villagers had grown their crops, or the common land, where their animals grazed. Those without land often moved to the towns, to search for work.

Some towns grew fast. London was by far the largest city in Britain. Its population grew from about 60,000 in 1500 to 200,000 in 1600. 'What city in the world so populous, so merchantable, more rich?' wrote an enthusiastic Londoner in 1596. London impressed all visitors with its size, but most towns in Tudor Britain were much smaller – about the size of a modern village. Norwich, in Norfolk, the second largest city in Britain after London, only covered one square mile, and a countryman coming to market could cross the city in a few minutes. It still had its medieval walls (as did at least 146 other towns in England and Wales), although some houses were beginning to spill out beyond them.

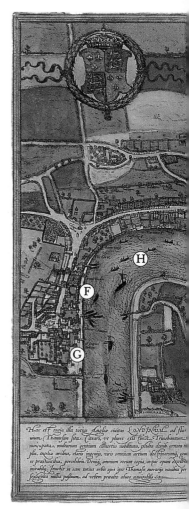

This picture map of London in 1572 shows the growing city spreading beyond the walls in Elizabethan times. The letters show the main landmarks.

A. The city of London surrounded by walls with seven gates.

B. The Tower of London.

C. St Paul's Cathedral. In 1561 lightning had destroyed its steeple 152 metres high, although it is still shown on this map.

D. London Bridge. Most trading ships tied up at Billingsgate, just before they reached the bridge. Above its main gateway the sailors would see the heads of executed criminals.

E. Southwark, the centre of entertainment: bull and bear-baiting, and theatres.

F. Whitehall, the main royal palace from 1530.

G. The city of Westminster, with the law-courts, the Palace of Westminster where Parliament usually sat, and the royal church, Westminster Abbey.

H. The river Thames, London's most important main highway, always full of boats.

'A stinking city, the filthiest of the world', wrote an experienced traveller, Sir Philip Hoby, about London in 1557. Dirt, as well as disease and fire, were day-to-day problems with which townspeople had to live, and try to control. In many towns officials had to make regulations again and again, so people cannot have taken much notice of them. In 1517 York City Council ordered that,

> No manner of person shall cast any manner of filth of hogs or dogs against Greyfriars Wall, but behind the new jetty.

and in Northampton, in 1535, the Butchers' Guild ordered that,

> No man… cast no manner of offal as lights, lungs, horns, and other annoyable things behind the stalls or on the pavement.

The Shambles, a street in York, still looks much as it did in medieval and Tudor times, although without the dirt. Butchers and tanners, whose work was particularly messy, usually worked in the Shambles, which explains our modern use of the word to mean disorder.

The daily round

A woman making butter in a wooden churn. It took a long time and was hard work.

A book of farming advice written in 1525 gives an enormous list of daily tasks for the farmer's wife. After starting her day with a prayer, she must sweep and tidy the house, milk the cows, get her children up, prepare meals for the household, bake bread, brew ale, make butter and cheese, look after the pigs and poultry, grow herbs and vegetables, and make sheets, towels and shirts. As if that were not enough, her distaff for spinning must always be ready, 'that thou be not idle ... help thy husband to fill the dung-cart, drive the plough, to load hay... and to go and ride to market.'

The great mass of men and women in Britain who worked with their hands to keep themselves alive hardly needed this kind of advice. They used the same tools and did the same tasks as they had done for centuries. Further up the social scale, Bess of Hardwick personally organized the building of her great house, Hardwick Hall, kept her accounts and ran her large household in the same way as a baron's wife would have done several centuries earlier.

By the end of the sixteenth century, houses and furniture, in both the town and the country, had become more comfortable for all except the very poor. Old men in William Harrison's Essex village told him how houses had improved since their younger days, especially for yeomen who had done well out of high food prices. Windows now had glass instead of dark and draughty wooden shutters. Fireplaces and chimneys had replaced smoking hearths in the middle of the room. Beds had soft feather mattresses instead of prickly straw, and pillows instead of a log. Plates and spoons were no longer made of wood, but of tin or pewter, and sometimes even silver.

Illness remained a part of everyday life, and there were few hospitals to care for the sick. Only the rich could afford doctors, whose treatments anyway often did more to hinder than help a cure. One modern historian thinks that people in the sixteenth century (and earlier too) were probably ill for about half of the time.

The diet of the rich must have affected their health. They ate a great deal of meat, often with rich sauces, and not much fruit and vegetables. They could also afford the expensive luxury of sugar. 'Pot herbs' (mostly peas, beans and onions), coarse bread and watery ale (there was no tea or coffee) was still the most usual meal for a villager. Although this sounds healthier, there was often too little of it. Since about one harvest in five failed during the sixteenth century, food shortages often lowered people's resistance to disease, which led to sickness and epidemics.

Bubonic plague seldom left Britain. Smallpox often seemed to hit the rich – Elizabeth I nearly died of it in 1562. Typhus, or 'camp fever', spread by body lice, attacked large groups especially armies on campaign.

This is part of a picture in the National Portrait Gallery in London, painted in about 1596 by an unknown artist. It shows the birth, life and death of an Elizabethan gentleman, Sir Henry Unton. On the right is his birth and education. In the centre, Sir Henry holds a feast in his house. At the top Sir Henry lies dying of a fever, with his servants weeping by his bedside. A physician, the top rank of doctor, is giving him the most up-to-date treatment: bleeding, and a medicine made from gold, musk and 'unicorn's horn'. It was all no use.

There were outbreaks of the 'sweating sickness', a killer influenza virus. In 1551 so many farm labourers died from it that 'in some places the corn stood and shed on the ground for lack of workmen'.

Childbirth was dangerous for both mothers and babies, and many children died, especially babies in their first year. For most people their lives were shorter than they are today. The old were the tough ones who survived. Warmer, more comfortable houses may have helped recovery from illness, and also cut down chest infections. This may also help to explain why the population continued to rise in spite of so much disease.

Nine out of ten people in the sixteenth century still lived and worked on the land, either in villages or in small scattered groups in the more distant uplands of the north and west of Britain. For them the daily round had altered little over the centuries. Nevertheless, the changing times described in the next few chapters would affect their everyday lives in many ways.

CHAPTER 2

Rival kings

❖

Henry VIII's subjects admired the talents of their dazzling Renaissance prince, but that was not enough for him. He wanted to win glory in war, especially against France, England's old enemy. Henry VIII and Francis I of France were rivals in magnificence – Henry even decided he had a better shaped leg than the French king. He also dreamed of winning back English lands lost in the Hundred Years War more than sixty years earlier, and was ready to risk trouble with England's other old enemy, Scotland, who in the past had so often allied with France against England.

This painting, called The Field of the Cloth of Gold, *shows the peacemaking ceremony in 1520, when Henry VIII met his rival the king of France. Henry arrives in procession, the two kings meet in a golden tent in the centre background, and on the far right they joust. The royal feasts and grandeur meant very little – the two kings were at war again two years later.*

The Mary Rose, *the King's second largest warship, ready for battle. She bristled with guns, poking out from the gunports along her sides, some very close to the waterline. On a calm July day in 1545, she capsized and sank near Portsmouth. The cause was probably the water gushing in through the lower gunports. The ship took down with her all her equipment and most of her crew of 600. Over 400 years later, archaeologists re-discovered this Tudor time capsule, and in 1982 the remains of the ship were hauled out of the sea.*

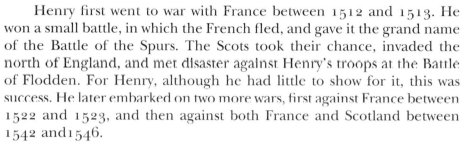

Henry first went to war with France between 1512 and 1513. He won a small battle, in which the French fled, and gave it the grand name of the Battle of the Spurs. The Scots took their chance, invaded the north of England, and met disaster against Henry's troops at the Battle of Flodden. For Henry, although he had little to show for it, this was success. He later embarked on two more wars, first against France between 1522 and 1523, and then against both France and Scotland between 1542 and 1546.

As well as the suffering brought by war, it was expensive. Fighting men needed equipment, as well as pay and food supplies. Even collecting enough carts to transport everything was often a problem. Iron-workers in Sussex worked overtime, and Henry's new armouries at Greenwich made battle armour as well as elaborately decorated jousting armour. Great warships were built in the new dockyards on the mouth of the river Thames at Deptford and Woolwich, and forts were constructed along the south coast as a defence against a French attack. By the end of his first French war, Henry had spent all the money his father left him. He continued to spend whether or not he had the money.

The power of the king

'The prince is the life, the head and the authority of all things that be done in the realm of England', wrote a councillor in 1565 about Tudor monarchs. The nobles and ministers at Henry's court competed with each other to gain the glittering prize of the king's favour, but he also needed their help. The most important nobles and bishops, as well as some men with talent who were less well-born, served him on his Council. As in earlier times, they gave him advice, carried out his orders, and sometimes managed to influence his decisions.

The king also had to depend on the landowners, who were so powerful in their own local areas, to keep control of the whole of his kingdom. There were no policemen in Tudor England, nor was there a royal army. Henry needed these 'ruling classes' to keep order in the area where they lived, to collect taxes and to raise troops when needed.

The king also decided when to call Parliament, which usually met at Westminster. When he did, it was for three reasons. First, and usually on his orders, the House of Commons and the House of Lords passed laws. They had to approve each 'Act of Parliament', and then the king gave his agreement, or assent. They usually passed the laws the king wanted, but they had the chance to criticize, and to suggest laws of their own, and they sometimes did.

Henry VIII on his throne in Parliament. He sits in the House of Lords, with bishops and abbots on the left, nobles on the right and judges in the centre. Members of the House of Commons (MPs, mainly landowners) are lined up at the bottom of the picture.

Second, the king usually asked Parliament to grant extra taxes. Since Henry spent an enormous amount of money on his palaces, ceremonies, banquets and wars, he always needed more. No-one likes taxes, and even under a king as intimidating as Henry, Parliament did not always co-operate. In 1523 Henry was only granted half the sum he demanded for his French war, and one MP grumbled: 'I have heard no man in my life that can remember that ever there was given to any one of the King's ancestors half so much at one grant'.

Third, by listening to MPs the king could learn through Parliament what was happening in different parts of the country. Although he was often difficult and harsh, Henry VIII had a knack of being in touch with his subjects. The ruling classes in Parliament could also sometimes make their opinions clear, but they also took care not to offend the king.

Thomas Wolsey, the king's servant

With so much to interest and entertain him, Henry was lucky that he soon found a servant he could trust to carry out the everyday routine of running the country. Thomas Wolsey was no ordinary court adviser. The son of a butcher from Ipswich in Suffolk, he rose to the top to be Lord Chancellor.

He began by first entering the Church. Being a churchman was still a good way for a bright boy from an ordinary family to get on in the world. He became not only Archbishop of York, but also held other rich bishoprics. The Pope first made him a Cardinal (the top rank of churchman) and then, in 1517, his Legate, the Pope's special representative in England.

In 1515 the king made him Lord Chancellor. Wolsey's work for the king left him little time for church affairs. Soon he was running most state matters, as well as answering the king's letters. He made summaries of long documents, 'because it should be painful to Your Grace to read the whole', while Henry hunted, jousted, made music or feasted.

The low-born Wolsey became one of the richest men in England, which most of the nobles at Henry's court deeply resented. He enjoyed grandeur as much as the king he served. One of his close attendants, George Cavendish, described how he would go in procession to the law courts each day in his crimson satin cardinal's robes, holding an orange stuffed with vinegar and herbs to his nose to protect him from the crowds of grubby people who pressed around him:

> Thus he passed forth, with two great crosses of silver borne before him … his mule trapped all together in crimson velvet, and gilt stirrups … with his cross bearers also upon great horses trapped in fine scarlet …

Wolsey made the most of his wealth, but he also encouraged learning. He founded a school in his home town of Ipswich, and a new college,

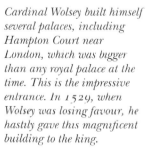

Cardinal Wolsey built himself several palaces, including Hampton Court near London, which was bigger than any royal palace at the time. This is the impressive entrance. In 1529, when Wolsey was losing favour, he hastily gave this magnificent building to the king.

The bulky figure of Thomas Wolsey in his Cardinal's robes, painted by an unknown artist when the Chancellor was at the height of his power.

now called Christ Church, at Oxford University. Cavendish also noted that his master was always a fair judge, sparing neither rich nor poor, and that 'whatever business or weighty matters he had in the day, he never went to his bed with any part of his divine service unsaid, yea not so much as one collect [prayer]'.

Wolsey served the king faithfully, and did his best, through arranging alliances with foreign powers, to make Henry important in Europe. Some historians have thought that his real aim was to be Pope, but it is more likely that he was trying, as always, to please Henry. Wolsey organized the great meeting with the king of France at the Field of the Cloth of Gold in 1520 (he is riding ahead of Henry on a grey mule in the picture on page 20). When Henry once again went to war against France in 1523, Wolsey arranged an alliance with the French king's great rival, the Emperor Charles V, who ruled Spain and the Netherlands, and the parts of Germany and Italy still called the Holy Roman Empire.

England was not rich and important enough to make these alliances last and, like Henry, Wolsey was more interested in spending money than collecting it. When in 1525 people in Norfolk and Suffolk rioted against a tax demanded without Parliament's consent, Wolsey had to take all the blame. The king must have agreed to the tax, but did not check the complaints of his jealous and hostile courtiers. It suited Henry to blame his minister if things went wrong, but for the moment Wolsey was useful to him.

The four nations of Britain

Henry VIII ruled not only the English but also the Welsh and the Irish and, like many English kings before him, he wanted to extend and strengthen his power over the whole of Britain, including the independent kingdom of Scotland.

Wales, Ireland and Scotland each had their own culture and language. They were poorer countries than England, and their ports were further away from the profitable European trade routes. All three were mountainous, with less fertile land and a wetter climate. Yet all could be a threat to England, each a back door through which enemies might attack.

The Welsh fiercely guarded whatever independence they had managed to keep since Edward I's conquest, and they resented the English. 'Those Saxons of false faith shall wade in their own blood up to their fetlocks!' a Welsh poet foretold hopefully in the 1480s. Like Welsh poets for centuries, he had trained for nine years in his craft. Poets and singers had an honoured place in the households of Welsh gentlemen, and did much to inspire the Welsh language.

The arrival on the throne of the Tudors, who came from Wales,

Wales after The Act of Union, 1536

- ▨ The counties of Wales
- ▨ The Marches, the border area controlled by the Council of Wales
- - - - boundary with England 1542–1830

0   25   50 km

gave the Welsh gentry more opportunity to do well in England, although they were not popular there. The English saw the Welsh as wild and lawless, mainly because English officials and law courts found it extremely difficult to impose English law in Wales. In 1534 a local official wrote despairingly to the government in London, 'I beg you to send down to us some man to use the sword of justice, otherwise the Welsh will war so wild, it will not be easy to bring them to order again'.

In 1536 the Act of Union strengthened English control over Wales. It divided the country into thirteen counties, organized like the English ones. English, not Welsh, had to be the language used in law courts and for all official business. Most Welsh landowners could now be Members of Parliament, own English land and take part in English affairs. Many of their sons had an English education – Shrewsbury School (1552) and Jesus College, Oxford (1571), were founded for them.

Ordinary Welsh-speaking people resented these changes most, for they could not always understand English officials, or English laws. The Welsh language suffered, especially as the invention of printing also brought into Wales a mass of books in English. Educated people became less interested in Welsh, and fewer of them spoke it.

In Ireland, the chiefs were still regarded as kings in the areas which they ruled. They and their people spoke the Irish language. English laws and customs were only obeyed in 'the Pale', an area of about eighty kilometres around Dublin, and the English king was only 'Lord of Ireland'.

The most powerful men in Ireland were the 'Old English', the descendants of Norman settlers. Chief among them was the Earl of Kildare. His son, 'Silken Thomas', had a bodyguard of armed men who swaggered round Dublin with silken trappings on their horses. They rebelled against the English in Henry VIII's crisis year of 1534. Henry crushed the rebellion and had Thomas executed. In 1541 Henry took the title of 'King of Ireland'. All the Irish chiefs now held their land from him, and had to obey English laws. Few did, but now English rulers claimed to own the whole of Ireland. Trouble lay ahead.

An English drawing of Irish kerns or soldiers, brandishing their swords and daggers. Their 'glibs' (wild locks of hair), tattered cloaks and bare feet seemed strange and barbarian to the English. An observer who wrote in 1515: 'There be more than sixty ... regions in Ireland, inhabited with the King's Irish enemies ... where reigneth more than sixty captains ... that liveth by the sword and ... maketh war and peace for himself.'

James the fourt Began His Rayne 1489 He maried Margaret eldest dochter of Henry the sebinth

James IV's marriage in 1502 to Margaret Tudor, Henry VIII's sister, linked England and Scotland closely, but not always peacefully. This picture was painted almost a hundred years later in 1600, just before their great grandson, James VI, became the first Stuart king of England.

James IV of Scotland

The Stuart king, James IV of Scotland (1488–1513), was, like Henry VIII, a man with many abilities and interests, another 'Renaissance prince'. He had a much more difficult start to his reign than the English king. James was only fifteen when he joined a rebellion in 1488 against his cruel and unjust father, James III, who was killed in the fighting.

Scots kings had to rule the 'wild Scots', the chiefs and their clans in the distant and barren Highlands, as well as the English-speaking 'household Scots' in the burghs (Scottish towns) and farms of the Lowlands. James IV learned how to control his unruly kingdom with skill.

James IV had wide interests. In 1508 he gave permission to the first Scots printers to set up their presses in Edinburgh. The University of Aberdeen was founded in his reign. Medicine fascinated him; he could pull out an aching tooth, and set a broken leg.

Although, like his brother-in-law Henry VIII, James spent money lavishly, he raised it by running the royal lands efficiently, and did not ask for unpopular taxes. His accounts show that, like the English king, he spent

large sums on the royal sports of hunting and jousting. He regularly paid the poet William Dunbar, and an Italian, John Damian, who claimed he could turn ordinary metal into gold.

James kept a magnificent court, to equal that of the English king. He built Holyrood Palace in Edinburgh, and the great hall at Stirling Castle. Like Henry, he spent most on war. He spent £30,000 on his great ship the *Michael*, and Henry copied the design in his own slightly smaller warships.

When Henry VIII first went to war against France, James decided to break the peace treaty he had made when he married Henry's sister Margaret. He set out to win a glorious victory by invading England. In September 1513, in driving wind and rain, the Scots and English armies clashed at Flodden just south of the Scots border. The battle was a disaster for the Scots. Three bishops, eleven earls and fifteen lords were killed, together with about 16,000 ordinary soldiers. After the battle, the body of James IV was found under a pile of Scottish corpses.

'Woe to the land that's governed by a child!' wrote William Shakespeare in his play *Richard III*. Scotland's next three rulers were each to inherit their crown as a baby. James IV's son was only a few months old when he became the new king in 1513. Later in his reign, James V (1513–1542) had to face an English invasion and another defeat, at Solway Moss. He was already ill when he heard of the disaster and it is said that when he was told he turned his face to the wall and died. His six-day-old baby daughter, Mary, now became queen. (Twenty-six years later, her son was crowned King James VI of Scotland, aged 13 months.) English armies burnt the city of Edinburgh, and remained on Scottish soil for several years. Yet with France as their ally, the Scots were stronger than they seemed and Henry VIII never became king of Scotland.

By 1542 the English king had a very different matter to occupy him. Since the late 1520s he had been in head-on collision with one of the most powerful and important men in Europe, the Pope in Rome. Henry was set on a course which would change the lives of all his people.

Stirling Castle, where James IV often held court. His favourite, John Damian, once tried to fly off the walls of the castle with homemade wings. He fell straight into a dung heap and broke his leg.

CHAPTER 3
Divided Christians

❖

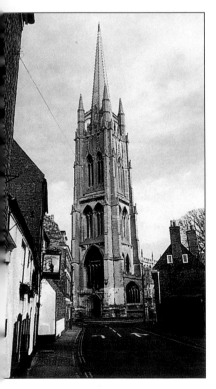

Local people often gave a great deal to their parish church. The steeple of Louth parish church in Lincolnshire took fourteen years to build and cost £305, a large sum for a small town to raise. It still soars into the sky, 100 metres high.

On 13 September 1515 the church bells were ringing in the little town of Louth in Lincolnshire, and the streets were full of people celebrating. The new steeple for the parish church was finished. After it had been blessed by the parish priest, 'the churchwardens garte [made] ring all the bells, and caused all the people … to have bread and ale, and all to the loving of God, Our Lady and All Saints.'

Just over twenty years later, in the autumn of 1536, Louth was a very different place. The town was full of ugly rumours. Already orders from Henry VIII and his minister Thomas Cromwell had cancelled most of the precious 'holy days', or saints' days, which were the only holidays people had. Cromwell's officials had closed some smaller monasteries nearby, and the king had seized their treasure and land. Would he take the treasures belonging to their parish church next? There were fears of new taxes as well. No one knew what might happen.

An angry crowd gathered when one of Cromwell's men arrived, and a brawl turned into a riot. The king's men soon crushed 'the most brute and beastly' Lincolnshire rebels, as Henry angrily called them, but a few weeks later most of the north of England flared up in rebellion. Its leaders called it the Pilgrimage of Grace.

The changes which upset people so much in the north of England in 1536 were part of a religious revolution in Europe, now called the Reformation. This split the Catholic Church, the biggest organization in western Europe, led by the Pope in Rome. In 1517 Martin Luther, a friar in Wittenberg, in the German state of Saxony, began to preach against the power of the Pope and priests, monks and nuns. Luther taught that the key to true religion was the Bible, which people should study for themselves in their own language. Luther's followers came to be called Protestants. (The word came from some German princes who supported Luther. In 1529 they published a 'Protest' against their Catholic emperor,

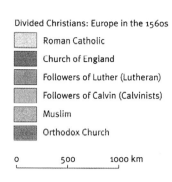

Divided Christians: Europe in the 1560s

- Roman Catholic
- Church of England
- Followers of Luther (Lutheran)
- Followers of Calvin (Calvinists)
- Muslim
- Orthodox Church

0   500   1000 km

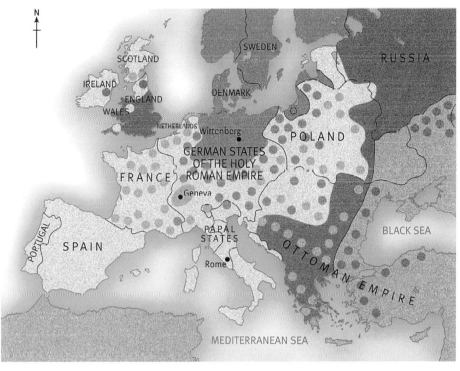

As the ideas of Luther and Calvin spread throughout Europe, so religious disagreement led to wars between rulers as they saw their power threatened. The followers of Calvin were called Huguenots in France, Presbyterians in Scotland and Puritans in England.

The church in South Leigh, Oxfordshire, still looks much as it did before the Reformation, with wall paintings and the rood (a statue of Jesus on the Cross) on the screen. Protestants believed statues and pictures encouraged superstition, so their churches were plainer. Calvin's churches had no altar, and the pulpit (where the preacher explained the Bible) was in the centre.

who had condemned Luther's teaching). The new printing presses spread Protestant ideas rapidly across northern Europe.

Different and more extreme Protestant groups began to emerge. The most powerful was led by Jean (or John) Calvin in Geneva in Switzerland from 1541. There, each church had its own minister and chose 'presbyters', or elders, to run its affairs. There were no bishops to give them orders. Calvin taught that true Christians, who believed that God had saved them from Hell, should lead strict lives without worldly luxuries. Calvin's teachings were often harsh, but his Church in Geneva also inspired people.

This Reformation bitterly divided Christians in Europe. The German states were torn apart by war as their Catholic emperor, Charles V, tried to defeat the princes who had become Protestants. From 1562, religious wars broke out in France and the Netherlands.

Protestant ideas began to reach England by the 1520s, mainly through trading links with the German states and the Netherlands, but it was a quarrel about a marriage, which at first had little to do with religion, that led to the English Reformation.

Henry VIII painted by his great court artist Hans Holbein, a few years after the divorce crisis in 1536. Holbein painted the king's rich clothes so cleverly that they look real, and used actual gold for the decoration and jewels. Henry was 44 by this time, already overweight, but still powerful, impressive and ruthless.

The king's 'Great Matter'

Henry VIII considered himself to be a good churchman. He had even written a book condemning the teachings of Martin Luther, and was delighted when the Pope rewarded him with a new title, Defender of the Faith. (The initials F.D. around the monarch's head on modern British coins still stand for this). Henry also usually got his own way, but for one matter. By 1527 he had been married to Catherine of Aragon for eighteen years, and still had no son. All the babies born to his queen had died

(right) Catherine of Aragon painted by an unknown artist in 1527, the year her marriage became doomed. She was popular, generous to the poor and admired for her learning and piety.

(far right) Anne Boleyn, also painted in about 1527, wearing the fashionable French hood which showed her glossy dark hair, in contrast to Catherine's heavy, old-fashioned Spanish head-dress. Anne was intelligent and sharp, and as strong a character as Catherine.

This beautiful book is the English translation of the New Testament by William Tyndale, printed in 1534. It belonged to Anne Boleyn, who was interested in Protestant ideas and supported the Bible in English.

except for one, a girl, Mary, who was now aged eleven. It was taken for granted that ruling was a man's job, and that the rule of a queen would lead to chaos.

Henry convinced himself that it was a sign of God's displeasure that he had no male heir. His marriage, he now believed, was not a true one, since Catherine had been married first to his brother Arthur, who had soon died. The king was also passionately in love with a court lady, Anne Boleyn. She was lively, well educated and twenty years younger than Catherine. Henry was determined to divorce Catherine and marry Anne. He called this his 'Great Matter', and could think of little else. But only the Pope could grant him the divorce he so much wanted.

Catherine, a strong-minded religious woman, insisted she was Henry's 'true wife'. She had one great advantage. Her nephew, the Emperor Charles V, had just conquered most of Italy and made the Pope his prisoner, and he was certainly not going to allow his aunt to be humiliated. So when Henry ordered his Chancellor, Thomas Wolsey, to persuade the Pope to grant the king's divorce, Wolsey had no success. Henry was ruthless with people who failed him, and in 1529 he dismissed Wolsey. The disgraced minister was soon accused of treason, and only escaped execution because he died on the way to his trial. As he lay dying, he said to the king's official:

> If I had served God as diligently as I have done the King, he
> would not have given me over in my grey hairs ... I warn you
> to be well advised ... what matter you put in his [the king's]
> head; for ye shall never pull it out again.

EARL OF ESSEX.

A good copy of Holbein's portrait of Thomas Cromwell, painted in 1533 when he had become the most powerful man on Henry's Council. He wears sober black, unlike the magnificent Wolsey, and has his writing materials by him as a reminder of his careful, efficient work organizing the king's affairs.

Supreme Head of the Church

Gradually a new idea was forming in Henry's head, and certainly no-one would pull it out again. He realized that if he, rather than the Pope, controlled the Church in England, it could grant his divorce, and he would not need the Pope. In 1532 he appointed a new Archbishop of Canterbury, Thomas Cranmer. Cranmer was a quiet and loyal scholar, interested in reforming the Church. Soon the need for action was urgent, for Anne Boleyn had become pregnant, and this child must surely be the long-awaited son and heir. There was a secret marriage early in 1533, and a few months later Archbishop Cranmer decreed that Henry's marriage to Catherine had never legally existed, and he crowned Anne queen. In September, to Henry's bitter disappointment, Anne gave birth to a daughter, Elizabeth.

Meanwhile, the king's efficient new minister, Thomas Cromwell, ensured that Henry had the extra powers he needed to become head of the English Church. In 1534, under Cromwell's guidance, Parliament recognized Henry as Supreme Head of the Church of England, with Anne as his rightful queen. Her children would succeed to the throne. All important people had to swear an oath accepting this.

The end of the monasteries

Although Henry VIII was Supreme Head of the English Church, he did not control a large part of it. Over 800 monasteries and nunneries in England and Wales still owed obedience to the Pope. They were also rich in land and treasure, and Henry was always short of money.

The king and Cromwell decided on the destruction of the monasteries. Cromwell laid his plans with care. First his officials investigated every religious house, determined to prove that monks and nuns were not keeping their vows and were superstitious and worldly. This report, on the important monastery of Bury St Edmund's, in Suffolk, shows what they were looking for:

> As for the abbot … he delighted in playing at dice and cards, and therein spent much money … there was here … women coming and resorting to this monastery … Amongst the relics we found much vanity and superstition, as the coals on which St Lawrence was toasted …, the paring of St Edmund's nails, St Thomas of Canterbury's penknife and his boots, and … skills [charms] for the headache.

The ruins of Tintern Abbey, on the Welsh border, whose lands the king granted to the Earl of Worcester, a leading Welsh landowner, to make sure he remained loyal. The king took the Abbey's treasure and land. Local people took much of the stone and other building materials. Once the valuable lead on the roof had gone, the building fell into ruin.

Some monastery churches were saved. In Tewkesbury in Gloucestershire, for example, the Abbey became the local parish church. The biggest ones, such as those at St Albans and Peterborough, became cathedrals.

Such reports gave the king and Cromwell what they wanted; a good reason to destroy the monasteries. In 1536 an Act of Parliament 'dissolved' the small monasteries. By 1539 even the largest monasteries had either given up their buildings and land of their own free will, or the inhabitants had been driven out.

The 'dissolution' of the monasteries had a huge effect on English society. Some monks and nuns had run schools, cared for the poor and sick, and provided hospitality for travellers, especially in the north. These services were not always very efficient, but the king did little to replace them.

Since Henry went on spending money at a vast rate, he sold a great deal of the land that had belonged to the monasteries. Landowners grabbed the chance to buy this valuable land and enlarge their estates. These nobles and gentry certainly did not want to see the monks and nuns return. This meant that it would now be very difficult to undo the changes Henry had made.

A Bible people could read

So far Henry VIII had done little to encourage the spread of Protestant beliefs in England – he had simply taken over the Church. In 1539 however he allowed Cromwell to organize the printing of the Bible in English, and every church was ordered to buy one. Since Protestants believed that everyone should be able to read the Bible in their own language, it seemed that the king was changing his mind.

Bible reading seems to have spread, especially in the towns where people had more chance to learn to read. By 1543 the king was so alarmed by this that he changed his mind again. He ordered Parliament to pass a law forbidding women, apprentices and labourers to read the Bible. It seems to have had little

The beautiful hand-written books in the medieval library of Hereford Cathedral are so valuable they have always been chained up. They have survived, but when Henry VIII seized other monastery libraries many priceless manuscripts were lost or sold.

Henry VIII made sure people knew who controlled the English Church when they opened the first page of the English Bible. The king sits at the top on his throne, and it is not so easy to see God above his head. Below him Cranmer and Cromwell hand out the Bible, and at the bottom the king's loyal subjects call out 'Vivat Rex' which is Latin for 'Long Live the King'.

effect. A Gloucestershire shepherd wrote this in another book he owned:

> I bought this book when the Testament [Bible] was abrogated [forbidden], that shepherds might not read it. I pray God amend that blindness. Writ by Robert Williams keeping sheep upon Seynbury Hill, 1546.

The English Bible was on its way to becoming the most important and influential book in the English language. Later, the Welsh had their own Bible. A Welsh vicar, William Morgan, spent six years translating the Bible into Welsh, and then another year in London supervising its printing by English workmen who did not understand the language. In 1588 his Welsh Bible was published. William Morgan's Bible not only inspired its readers, but also helped to keep the Welsh language alive.

God's servants

In the sixteenth century, people believed that their king had been placed over them by God, and that they should obey him. Most of Henry's subjects swore the oath accepting him as Supreme Head of the Church, and it was very dangerous to risk the king's anger by refusing to take it.

Although Henry had made Sir Thomas More his Chancellor when Wolsey fell in 1529, More believed the king could not make himself head of the Church of God. He soon refused to swear the oath and resigned. Even after spending seventeen months in a cold, damp cell in the Tower of London, he still stood out against the king. When he was finally executed, he said on the scaffold, 'I die the King's good servant, but God's servant first.'

By 1536 many of Henry's subjects, like those in Louth, were deeply worried by the changes in the Church. As the north blew up in the rebellion called the Pilgrimage of Grace, the rebel leader Robert Aske's main demand was that the power of the Pope, as well as the monasteries, should be restored.

Henry summoned Aske and other rebel leaders to London and, after they had agreed to send their supporters home, he pretended to listen to their case. Then he pounced. Aske was hung in chains from the walls of York castle, and left to die in agony. Nearly 200 rebels were executed. There was no more trouble from the north.

Robert Aske was a deeply religious man. As he told his followers, he believed the rebellion he led was a 'Pilgrimage of Grace ... for the love that ye do bear to Almighty God ... to Holy Church, and to the preservation of the King's person.' This is a badge of the rebels representing the five wounds which Jesus suffered on the cross.

The king and his wives

The story of Henry VIII's six wives is closely linked to the story of the changes in the English Church. By the time Catherine of Aragon died in 1536, Henry's feelings towards Anne had cooled, especially as she had recently given birth to a dead son. She was accused of being unfaithful, probably falsely, and executed with a sword, as a sign of 'mercy'. The king then sent her two-year-old daughter Elizabeth away from court.

Jane Seymour was quiet and modest, quite the opposite of Anne. The Seymours were an ambitious Protestant family already in favour at court, and when the king married Jane immediately after Anne's execution, their influence grew. Jane gave Henry his longed-for son, Edward, in 1537 but she died twelve days later.

In 1540 Cromwell organized Henry's fourth marriage, to Anne of Cleves, a German princess, as part of an alliance with some German Protestant princes. Henry soon tired of the German alliance, and divorced Anne, saying she looked like a 'Flanders mare', a thickset farm horse. Then Cromwell's enemies at court brought about his fall. Henry's hard-headed, efficient minister was executed a month later.

(right) Jane Seymour, Henry VIII's third wife, who gave him the son he had wanted for so long. Holbein's picture shows her standing primly in her rich clothes and jewellery, and seems to fit her motto 'Bound to obey and serve.'

(far right) This richly dressed court lady may be Catherine Howard, Henry's ill-fated fifth wife.

(above) The German princess Anne of Cleves, painted by Holbein just before her short marriage to Henry in 1540.

(below) Edward VI, son of Jane Seymour. This portrait was painted after he became king, when he was about ten.

On the day that Cromwell was beheaded, Henry married Catherine Howard. She was the young niece of the powerful Duke of Norfolk, a Catholic who, although he had accepted Henry as Supreme Head of the Church, had worked against Cromwell, and opposed Protestant changes in the Church. Henry soon regretted the loss of Cromwell, who had served him faithfully for eight years, and he regretted this marriage too. Catherine was foolish enough to be unfaithful to the unhealthy, irritable old king, and she was executed in 1543.

The king's last choice was Catherine Parr, a sensible widow and probably a Protestant. She looked after the elderly king and his three children, who by this time were all back at court, and she outlived Henry.

The boy king

When the powerful and often terrifying Henry VIII died in 1547, his ministers did not dare to announce the fact for three days. His son, Edward VI (1547–1553), a serious, clever boy, was only nine years old. There were wars in France and Scotland, and massive royal debts.

Although Henry had broken the power of the Pope, he had not altered the Catholic church services, and many people felt as confused as the Catholic who wrote: 'The King was like one who would throw a man from a high tower, and bid him stay where he was half way down.'

Edward's uncle, the Duke of Somerset, seized power and declared himself Protector of the boy king. Arrogant and inefficient, he was pushed aside in 1549 by the ruthless and efficient John Dudley, who took the title of Duke of Northumberland and had Somerset executed in 1552.

Both these men were Protestants, and made this a good excuse to grab more property and treasure from the Church. Parish churches began to look very different, as wall paintings were covered with whitewash, and stained glass windows and statues were destroyed.

Meanwhile, Archbishop Thomas Cranmer set out to make a 'middle way' between Catholic and Protestant. He wrote a Prayer Book in clear English, but kept the order of the old services. An Act of Parliament in 1549 ordered Cranmer's Prayer Book to be used in every church. People missed the familiar Latin services even though they did not understand them. Rebellions broke out in Devon and Cornwall. The rebels called the new service 'a Christmas game' and condemned 'this new English'.

Only a few weeks later rebellion erupted in Norfolk led by Robert Ket, a prosperous tradesman. This rising was mainly against unpopular local landowners rather than for religious reasons. Indeed Ket and his followers used Cranmer's Prayer Book.

Both rebellions were ruthlessly crushed, as Northumberland took power. But his position, and Cranmer's Protestant changes, were soon threatened. By 1553, Edward, now sixteen years old, was desperately ill. It may have been his idea to ignore his Catholic half-sister, Mary, and leave the crown to his fifteen-year-old Protestant cousin, Lady Jane Grey. Northumberland saw his chance to survive and, backed by Jane's ambitious parents, forced her to marry his son, Lord Guildford Dudley.

When Edward died, in July 1553, Jane was proclaimed queen. She ruled for only nine days. As Mary marched to London to claim her throne, people flocked to support her as the rightful ruler. Northumberland was executed. Jane, the victim of other people's greed for power, was beheaded the following year with her young husband, when she was just seventeen.

It used to be thought that this portrait was of Lady Jane Grey. However, experts have found that the crown-shaped jewel she is wearing belonged to Catherine Parr, Henry VIII's sixth wife. The picture was painted in 1543, soon after Catherine's marriage to the King. Lady Jane Grey was only nine at the time.

A Catholic queen

Mary (1553–1558) was now thirty-seven years old, devoted to the memory of her mother, Catherine of Aragon, and determined to bring back the Catholic faith. Everyone expected her to marry, and she had no doubts about her choice: Philip, heir to the throne of Spain, the most powerful Catholic country in Europe. She hoped desperately for a son, so that her half-sister Elizabeth, the daughter of Anne Boleyn and probably Protestant, would no longer be her heir.

Many of Mary's subjects disliked this Spanish marriage, and feared England would be dragged into Spanish affairs. There was a brief but threatening rebellion in Kent, but the wedding went ahead, and Mary set about restoring both the Catholic Church and the Pope's power in England.

Back came pictures, statues of saints and relics in church, although very few monks and nuns returned, and landowners were allowed to keep their monastery lands. The queen and her bishops believed they must stamp out Protestant beliefs. About 800 Protestants, mostly richer people who could afford the journey, fled abroad to Calvin's Geneva and Protestant cities in the German states. From 1554 Protestants in England were hunted down, and nearly 300 were burned as heretics, mostly in the south-east where Protestant beliefs were strongest.

Although people were used to public executions, Mary's burnings were unpopular. This was probably because, apart from four bishops, most of the victims were as ordinary as the crowds who watched them die – weavers, cobblers, farm labourers, and at least fifty women.

Mary's reign lasted only five years, not long enough to restore the Catholic Church securely. Her marriage brought her no happiness, for Philip of Spain soon left the country. England was dragged into a war between Spain and France, which led to the loss of Calais, her last remaining possession in Europe. Bad harvests and a killer influenza epidemic in 1557 increased the gloom. To Mary's great grief, she never bore a son. She died in 1558, a sad, disappointed woman, knowing that her Protestant half-sister Elizabeth would rule after all, and probably undo her work.

CHAPTER 4

Queen and people

❖

Princess Elizabeth, aged thirteen. She holds a book to emphasize her learning, and perhaps to display her fine hands. She probably referred to this portrait when she wrote to her brother Edward in 1547, 'For the face I grant you I may well blush to offer, but the mind I shall never be ashamed to present.'

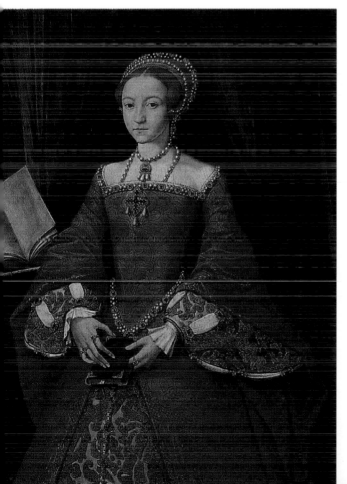

Elizabeth I was clever, quick-witted and well-educated. She could read Latin and Greek and spoke French and Italian fluently. Her childhood had not been happy. She was two years old when her mother, Anne Boleyn, was executed and she then had four stepmothers. She was imprisoned by her elder sister Queen Mary, who never trusted her. Elizabeth learned early to be cautious and hide her feelings.

As the new queen rode into London in November 1558, an observer noticed how cleverly she won the affection of the cheering crowds: 'Her eye was set upon one, her ear listened to another … her spirit seemed to be everywhere… distributing her smiles, looks, and graces'.

In spite of her welcome in London, for many people Elizabeth was another woman ruler who faced great difficulties which she was unlikely to be able to solve. One of her councillors wrote:

> The Queen poor, the realm exhausted … the people out of order … Wars with France and Scotland. The French King bestriding the realm with one foot in Calais and the other in Scotland …

It certainly looked as if the country was poor. Bad harvests, food shortages and the costs of war pushed up prices, so times were hard for many of the queen's subjects. However, under both Mary and Elizabeth, ministers looked after the royal money carefully. Only when war returned in the 1580s did the crown begin to have serious money problems. Unlike her father, Elizabeth hated spending money. She built no new palaces and the rich velvets, silks and jewels in her gleaming dresses were used several times

These virginals (a small keyboard instrument) probably belonged to Elizabeth. The Scots ambassador to London described how he heard the queen play the virginals 'excellently well', although she stopped as soon as she realized he was listening, and pretended to slap him, saying she 'was not used to play before men, but when she was solitary, to shun melancholy.'

over. Once she even ordered her soldiers to pick up the cannon balls they had fired and use them again.

Elizabeth's subjects were 'out of order' mainly because the violent changes in the Church confused and divided them. Like Thomas Cranmer, Elizabeth hoped most of her subjects would accept the Church of England as a 'middle way' between Protestants and Catholics. An Act of Parliament in 1559 abolished the Pope's power and declared the queen to be 'Supreme Governor of the Church of England'. A new version of Cranmer's Prayer Book was issued and people had to attend Prayer Book services on Sunday by law. If they did not, they were fined twelve pence – a small sum for a landowner, but about two days' wages for a villager.

At first, Elizabeth's church just seemed to be one more change which might not last. Catholics often went to the new services to avoid trouble, but then held a secret Mass at home. When a Yorkshire woman was in trouble for not attending church, she protested that 'things are not in the Church as it hath been in her forefathers' days'. Many agreed with her.

Protestant landowners and clergy who had escaped into exile during Mary's reign now returned, full of enthusiasm to bring about a true Protestant Church in England at last. Many had been inspired by Calvin's church in Geneva (see page 29).They were soon nicknamed Puritans, because they wanted to 'purify' Elizabeth's Church of England of anything which seemed Catholic. For them a 'middle way' was not enough.

Elizabeth was determined not to allow any more confusing changes in religion. She was luckier than her half-sister Mary, for her reign lasted forty-five years, long enough for her changes to the Church of England to take root. People gradually accepted them and some at least became loyal to the 'middle way'.

The marriage game

Everyone expected Elizabeth to marry, to provide an heir and 'to relieve her of those labours which are only fit for men', as Philip II of Spain wrote when he was considering marrying Elizabeth in 1559. The queen cleverly used the possibility that she might marry, in her dealings with foreign countries and in controlling her courtiers at home.

At first the French king was the enemy 'bestriding the realm', because he had recently captured Calais and had strong influence in Scotland.

So, as she needed Spain's friendship, she appeared interested in Philip II's proposal. By 1578, however, Spain was a great danger. For a time, in spite of her subjects' disapproval, the queen seemed serious about marrying the Duke of Anjou, the king of France's brother, although she was over forty and the duke was so ugly that she nicknamed him her 'frog'.

Elizabeth must have realized how difficult it was for a Tudor queen to find a husband whom her people would accept. Foreigners were unpopular, and an English noble would cause jealousy at home. Yet if she did not marry and have children, she would have no direct heir to succeed her. She firmly refused to discuss the matter. Perhaps she showed her real feelings about marriage when she once angrily told her favourite, the Earl of Leicester, who had tried to give orders to one of her servants, 'I will have a mistress here, and no master.'

Ruling the country

Robert Dudley, painted in 1572, after the queen had made him Earl of Leicester. He was 'a very goodly person, tall and singularly well-featured', and perhaps the man Elizabeth really wanted to marry, although he often displeased her and was unpopular at court. When she died, the letter he had written to her just before his death in 1588 was found among her things. On it she had written, 'His last letter'.

Burghley House in Lincoln-shire, built by William Cecil, Lord Burghley, is one of the most impressive Elizabethan houses still standing today. Cecil made plenty of money in the queen's service and like many rich Elizabethans he spent a great deal on building. His other great house, Theobalds in Hertfordshire, was the wonder of the age, but it has not survived.

Elizabeth knew it was important to choose her advisers with care, and not to be influenced by her personal feelings. At the beginning of her reign she chose the experienced William Cecil to be her chief adviser and Secretary of State. Cecil had served Edward VI's Duke of Northumberland and, although he was Protestant, had managed to avoid trouble in Mary's reign. Elizabeth told him:

This judgment I have of you, that you will not be corrupted by any manner of gift, and that you will be faithful to the state, and that without respect of my private will, you will give me that counsel which you think best.

Elizabeth was right about Cecil, and he remained the most important adviser on her Council for the next forty years. She made him Lord Burghley in 1572. She relied on his advice, and during his last illness she sat with him and fed him herself.

Like other rulers before her, Elizabeth also had to call Parliament when she needed money. Then the nobles in the House of Lords and MPs in the House of Commons could try to influence her. She often tried to stop them discussing important matters, particularly religion (especially Puritan demands for changes in the Church) and her marriage. When Parliament begged her to marry in 1566, she angrily told them to mind their own business: 'I have as good a courage ... as ever my father had. I am your anointed queen.' But she tactfully asked for less money and promised to marry when it was 'convenient'. It never was.

Although MPs had the right to speak freely in Parliament, Elizabeth always had the final word, because she alone could summon and dismiss Parliament. There were only ten Parliaments in her reign of forty-five years.

The sixteen-year-old Mary Queen of Scots at the time of her marriage to the future king of France. She was tall and red-haired, and very popular at the French court.

Danger from Scotland

Although many English Catholics were loyal, some never accepted Elizabeth, the daughter of Anne Boleyn, as their rightful queen. They supported her Catholic cousin Mary Queen of Scots, the grand-daughter of James IV and Margaret Tudor (see page 26).

Mary had become queen of Scotland as a small baby. After an English victory over the Scots at Pinkie in 1547, the five-year-old queen was sent to the safety of the French court, while her mother ruled Scotland for her. By 1559 she was married to King Francis II of France. Mary was therefore a great danger to Elizabeth. She was queen of Scotland and France, and she had a claim to the English throne.

Then, suddenly, in December 1560, Francis II died of an ear infection. Mary, aged nineteen, had to leave the France she loved. On a grey August day in 1561 she returned to a divided Scotland, which she did not know at all. In 1560 Scots Protestant nobles had set up a Presbyterian 'Kirk' (Church) inspired by Calvin's Church in Geneva, but in the remote Highlands the Gaelic clansmen remained strongly Catholic.

Mary, unlike Elizabeth, hoped marriage would solve her problems as she tried to govern her unruly kingdom. Her choice of a second husband proved disastrous. The handsome Scots noble, Henry Darnley, turned out to be a weak, vain drunkard. The unhappy queen spent most of her time with her Italian musician and secretary, David Riccio, which made Darnley and other nobles extremely jealous. In March 1566, Mary was holding a supper party in Holyrood Palace when a group of nobles burst in, with Darnley lurking in the background. They dragged the terrified Riccio out of the room, and stabbed him.

Soon after Riccio's brutal murder, Mary gave birth to a son, James, and seemed to make it up with Darnley. But she had come to rely increasingly on one Protestant noble, the Earl of Bothwell. On 9 February 1567, Mary went out, leaving Darnley alone in a house in Edinburgh, called Kirk o' Field. Suddenly there was a huge explosion. In the garden of the ruined house Darnley and his servant were found strangled.

Many people believed that Bothwell had planned Darnley's murder, and that Mary knew this. But she did nothing to clear her favourite's name. Bothwell divorced his wife, carried Mary off and, only five months after Darnley's murder, married her in a Protestant ceremony.

By this time most of Mary's subjects had had enough. There was a rebellion, and Mary was forced to give up her throne. Her baby son was crowned King James VI. Bothwell escaped to Denmark, where he died miserably in prison. In 1568 Mary escaped from Scotland, fleeing over the border into England.

Threats at home

Elizabeth now faced a very difficult situation. She disapproved of subjects who rebelled against their ruler, especially one who was her cousin. If she sent Mary back to Scotland, it might be to her death. Yet if she allowed her to go to France, French help might make her a danger again. So she imprisoned the Scots queen in England. This was also dangerous, since some English Catholics began plotting to put her on the throne.

The following year, a serious rebellion broke out in the north of England, mainly supported by Catholics. It was cruelly put down but in 1570 the Pope, to inspire the English Catholics, made things far worse by issuing a Bull (an official proclamation) declaring that the queen was, 'deprived of her pretended title to the kingdom ... and we do command and charge all ... subjects ... not to obey her orders ... and laws.'

English and Welsh Catholics were now in a terrible position, for they had to choose between their religion and their queen. Although only a few Catholics were plotters, harsh new laws made things difficult for all of them. Fines for non-attendance at Church of England services increased from twelve pence to a crippling twenty pounds, and by 1585 it was treason, punished by death, to be a Catholic priest, or even to give a priest shelter. About 180 Catholics were executed under these laws in Elizabeth's reign. Like the Protestants burnt in Mary Tudor's reign, they believed they were dying for their faith. Elizabeth's councillors thought they were stamping out dangerous traitors.

For nineteen years Mary Queen of Scots was a prisoner in England, and a threat to Elizabeth. Parliament begged the queen to execute 'the monstrous huge dragon', but for a long time she put off the decision. By 1586 there was a network of government spies to trap Catholics. One uncovered a plot, led by a rash young Catholic, Anthony Babington, to murder Elizabeth. The spy produced a letter from Mary apparently agreeing to the plan. With this evidence, Elizabeth had to agree at last that Mary should be put on trial for treason. The verdict was guilty.

On a cold February morning in 1587, the Scots queen was beheaded in Fotheringay Castle, Northamptonshire. When Elizabeth heard that Mary was dead, 'she gave herself over to grief ... shedding abundance of tears'. The queen's sorrow may have been real. She also knew that Mary's execution would increase the threat from abroad.

The Spanish Armada

Religion divided the Catholic King Philip II of Spain from the Protestant Elizabeth, but there were also other reasons why England and Spain became bitter enemies. By the mid-sixteenth century Spain had won an empire in the 'New World' of America. Spanish galleons sailed home with treasure-loads of gold, silver, precious stones, expensive dyes and sugar (still a rare luxury in Europe). English sailors wanted a share of this rich trade, and their attacks on Spanish treasure ships increased. After an attack by Sir John Hawkins in 1569 a report from Spain complained that, 'the Queen pretends that all has been done without her knowledge and consent.'

Since 1567 Philip II had been trying to put down a rebellion (mainly by Protestants) in the Netherlands, which was part of the Spanish Empire. Elizabeth was slow to help the Protestant Dutch because she saw them as rebels and, at first, did not want to upset Philip. However, when Philip sent the Duke of Parma with the best army in Europe to the Netherlands, Elizabeth decided she had to do something. An English army arrived in

This miniature picture of the sailor and explorer, Sir Francis Drake, was painted soon after he returned in 1580 from an adventurous three-year journey around the world. He brought back five packhorse-loads of Spanish treasure, and Elizabeth knighted him on board his ship The Golden Hind.

1585. Although it achieved little, the exasperated Spanish king decided that in order to crush the Netherlands, he must first defeat the English.

As Philip built his Armada, a huge invasion fleet, news came in 1587 of the execution of Mary Queen of Scots. Philip was deeply shocked, but Mary's death also helped him, for before she died, she had passed on to him her claim to the English throne.

Two months after Mary's death English ships led by Sir Francis Drake sailed into Cadiz harbour catching the Spanish fleet unawares.

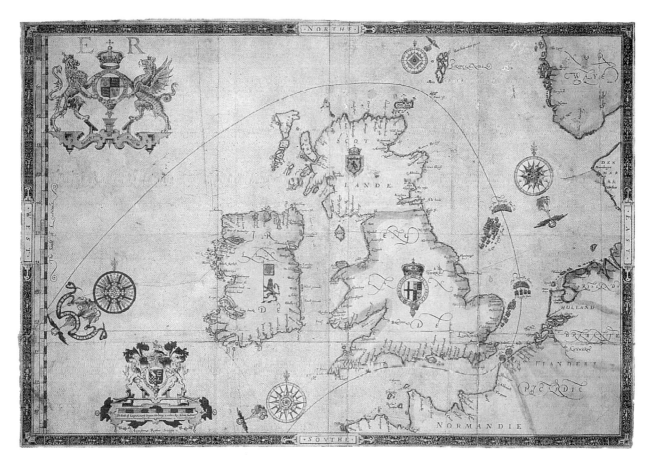

A chart of the Armada's route, dated 1590. While the English ships chased the Armada up the Channel, the Spaniards held their ships in a crescent formation. The heavy supply ships were in the centre, protected by the big galleons on the outer rim and tips, to deal with enemy attacks. The galleons aimed to close in and, using grappling irons, fasten themselves on to the English ships. They carried many soldiers on board for this fighting at close quarters.

Shipwrights plan the building of a warship. This picture illustrates some notes on ship design, written in about 1586 by Elizabeth's much respected master shipwright, Matthew Baker.

Drake claimed he destroyed thirty-seven ships and boasted that he had, 'singed the King of Spain's beard.' But beards grow again. Philip rebuilt his fleet, and in spite of serious shortages of food and other supplies, the Armada set sail in May 1588.

Philip ordered the Armada to sail to the Netherlands, join up with the Duke of Parma's army, and protect the barges which would carry this invasion force to England. He ignored the fact that there were no harbours in the Netherlands deep enough for his great ships. He also expected English Catholics to rise and help the Spanish forces.

The English waited uneasily for the invasion, trying to keep their ships supplied and ready for battle. At last, on 19 July 1588, the great crescent of 130 Spanish ships appeared on the horizon, off the coast of Cornwall. Beacons were lit from hilltop to hilltop across England, to call out troops from every county.

An English painting of the Spanish Armada as an evil crescent-shaped dragon, made about twenty years after the battle of 1588 and hung in a small village church in Lincolnshire. Pictures like this increased most English people's hatred and fear of Catholics, who were seen as supporters of a foreign enemy, even though they had stayed loyal in 1588.

The two fleets fought a running battle up the Channel, but the English ships could not break the strong Spanish crescent. On 27 July the Armada anchored off Calais, to try to make contact with Parma. The English sent in 'hellburners', blazing ships packed with gunpowder, a terrible threat to wooden fighting ships. As the Spaniards cut their anchors to take quick avoiding action, the crescent formation was broken at last.

For six days the two fleets battered each other. As the English ran out of ammunition and turned for home, gale force winds blew the damaged Spanish ships, full of wounded and sick men, steadily northwards round Scotland. Probably forty-four ships were wrecked on the treacherous rocky coasts of Scotland and Ireland. The rest limped home as best they could.

At first, the English did not know the danger was past. Elizabeth rode among her waiting troops at Tilbury, near London, and in a fiery speech told them:

> I am … resolved in the midst and heat of the battle to live or die amongst you all … I know I have the body of a weak and feeble woman, but I have the heart and stomach of a King, and of a King of England too, and think foul scorn that Parma, or Spain, or any prince of Europe should dare to invade the borders of my realm.

The enthusiastic but ill-trained troops never had to fight. There was no Catholic rising. For the English, the defeat of the Armada was a great victory, which saved them from a Spanish Catholic conquest. For Philip, it was only a setback. The war dragged on, another Armada was built, and clashes between English and Spanish ships continued.

Hard times in Ireland

Although Henry VIII had made himself 'King of Ireland', the Irish and the 'Old English' never accepted his break with the Pope. There were only a few Protestants in Ireland, mostly around Dublin. Both Catholic Mary and then Protestant Elizabeth tried to enforce English control by making grants of Irish land called 'plantations' to English settlers. In return for their land, the settlers had to agree to strict rules, which they did not always obey: they had to build a stone house and provide armed men for defence. To encourage them to bring in more English people, the settlers were not supposed to rent their land to the Irish, or to have Irish servants.

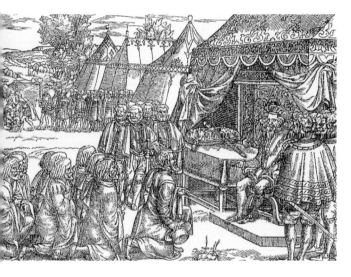

After their defeat in Ulster in 1603, Irish chiefs submitted to the English Lord Deputy on their knees. But they kept their Irish dress and flowing hair, their customs and their language. Once, when O'Neill was asked to speak English, one of his followers protested: 'Thinkest thou that it standeth with the O'Neill his honour to writhe his mouth in clattering English?'

There were six rebellions against English rule in Ireland in Elizabeth's reign. The most serious, in 1595, was led by Hugh O'Neill of Ulster, Earl of Tyrone. It became a seven years' national war, and was backed by Spain. O'Neill was finally defeated six days after Elizabeth's death in 1603. The chiefs lost their power, but the Irish people stubbornly held on to their customs, language and Catholic faith.

The cost was enormous on both sides. Elizabeth spent £2 million on O'Neill's war. As well as English soldiers, over 6000 Welsh soldiers fought there, and many died. The Irish people suffered terribly, mainly from famine. Even the English poet Edmund Spenser was shocked by the people he saw in Munster in 1596,

Out of every corner of the woods and glens they came creeping forth upon their hands, for their legs would not bear them … they spake like ghosts crying out of their graves.

Elizabethan entertainments

Towards the end of the sixteenth century, going to the theatre in Elizabethan London was new and fashionable. Earlier, people had watched plays performed in the street or inn-yards. In Elizabeth's reign several new theatres were built, including the famous Globe in London which was finished in 1599. A young actor, William Shakespeare, wrote most of the plays performed there. He excited and inspired the noisy audiences with romance, tragedy, blood and thunder, and knockabout comedy, as well as pride in their nation which had defeated the Armada. His plays also pleased the queen when she watched them at court.

Elizabethans enjoyed entertaining themselves, especially with music. In country houses, guests and servants would join in singing madrigals, songs written in several different parts for different voices. We know less

A sketch of the Swan Theatre, built in 1595 in London and very like Shakespeare's Globe theatre. It had no roof, and the stage jutted out into the audience. There was little scenery. Women did not act – boys took the female roles. Ordinary Londoners, the 'groundlings', stood at ground level in the open, whatever the weather. Seats in the covered galleries round the sides cost more.

In 1995 a new Globe theatre was opened in Southwark, in London, near the site of the original Globe. Although there is no picture of the original theatre, actors and builders used archaeological remains, this picture of the Swan, the plays and other evidence to re-create a building which is as close to Shakespeare's theatre as possible.

about how ordinary people enjoyed themselves, but there must have been many rowdy village festivities, such as the Christmas one described here by a disapproving Puritan in 1583:

> The wildheads of the parish … bedeck themselves with scarves, ribbons, and laces … they tie about either leg twenty or forty bells, with rich handkerchiefs in their hands … Then march these heathen company towards the church and churchyard, their pipers piping, their drummers thundering, their stumps dancing, their bells jingling, their handkerchiefs swinging above their heads like madmen, their hobby horses and other monsters skirmishing amongst the crowds.

The last years

The last years of Elizabeth's reign were harsh. As the expensive war with Spain and rebellion in Ireland dragged on, food prices rose sharply. Returning soldiers and sailors added to the many already seeking work. Even the climate seemed to get worse. From 1592 four cold wet summers brought four bad harvests, with two terrible years of famine.

Before Henry VIII closed down the monasteries, monks and nuns had sometimes cared for the poor. Now that they had gone, it was gradually realized that help must be properly organized in each parish.

In many towns, and some bigger villages, landowners and businessmen set up almshouses like these in Ewelme, Oxfordshire. They would provide food and shelter for the poor. In 1570 in Norwich (one of the largest cities in Britain at this time) the leading citizens made a list of families, like this one, who needed help: 'John Findley of the age of 82 years, cooper [barrel maker] not in work, and Joan his wife, sickly, that spin and knit'.

Landowners and prosperous merchants in the towns were afraid that the increasing numbers of those without work would cause trouble.

Gradually some richer people began to realize that those who were poor were not always idle, drunken troublemakers, but that sickness, old age and bad luck could cause poverty. Parliament made 'Poor Laws' to provide help. By 1601 each parish had to care for its own poor. To pay for this care, local people had to pay a tax called a rate. The new system was an improvement, but it still depended on the generosity of local people, and parish officials were still likely to push ragged and hungry 'strangers' out of their parish to become someone else's problem.

Elizabeth herself faced many difficulties in her last years. In 1601, her favourite, the Earl of Essex, rebelled against her, and she had to agree to his execution. In the same year, her last Parliament bitterly criticized her methods of raising money without their consent. They particularly disliked the sales of monopolies as rewards to courtiers. If a courtier bought a monopoly from the crown it meant that he alone had the right to sell or manufacture certain goods. Many everyday articles like salt, fish and coal became more expensive as a result. Yet Elizabeth still knew how to win her people's support. She promised her MPs she would abolish monopolies. Then she told them, in what became known as her Golden Speech:

Elizabeth I with her courtiers, painted in about 1600. The Earl of Worcester, one of the biggest landowners in Wales, probably ordered this picture, to please the queen and show his own important position at court. He is standing in the centre, near the queen, splendidly dressed in pink silk.

Though God hath raised me high, yet this I count the glory of my crown, that I have reigned with your loves … And though you have had, and may have, many princes more mighty and more wise sitting in this seat, yet you never have had nor shall have any that will be more careful and loving.

Even when she was old, Elizabeth enjoyed going on a progress with her court to see and be seen by her subjects. These visits to the houses of her nobles, or to cities such as Norwich, Oxford and Bristol also saved her money as her hosts paid the vast bills for food and entertainment. Lord Burghley built his huge house at Theobalds to entertain the queen. Each visit cost him about £3000 and Elizabeth went thirteen times.

The queen kept tight control of her portraits. Artists were only supposed to paint her if they used an approved face pattern. In the picture on page 49, she rides high above her courtiers. Her shimmering white dress is ablaze with jewels and although she was nearly seventy, her face shows no signs of age. She is shown as a goddess, 'Gloriana', who might rule for ever, so that her subjects could forget that she was in fact an old woman without an heir, who wore thick white make-up and a red wig.

In the cold spring of 1603, Elizabeth seemed to lose her will to live. She sat on cushions on the floor, sighing heavily and refusing to take any food or medicine. After four days she was coaxed into bed. As she lay dying, with the Archbishop of Canterbury holding her hand, some said she mumbled the name of the next ruler – James VI of Scotland, the son of Mary Queen of Scots.

An unusually realistic picture of the impressive old queen by Isaac Oliver, painted about 1590. It was almost certainly unfinished because Elizabeth disapproved of it. A German visitor who saw her in 1598 wrote: 'Next came the Queen… very majestic; her face oblong, fair but wrinkled; her eyes small, yet black and pleasant; her nose a little hooked; her lips narrow, and her teeth black … She had in her ears two pearls, with very rich drops; she wore false hair, and that red'.

CHAPTER 5

The path to war

❖

James VI of Scotland (1567–1625) lost no time in claiming his English crown. Three days after Elizabeth's death on 24 March 1603 a messenger from the English court reached Edinburgh. By 7 April James had crossed the border to become James I, the first Stuart king of England (1603–1625).

James was very different from the dignified, impressive Elizabeth. Although he was warmly welcomed by his subjects, he hated crowds. Court ceremonies often ended in a drunken muddle. He was lazy, especially after he came to England. He showered money and gifts on his favourites, who, at first, were mostly Scottish. A jealous English courtier, Anthony Weldon, made the most of his bad points, saying James was so terrified of being murdered that he wore heavily padded clothes. He added that,

his beard was very thin; his tongue too large for his mouth, which ... made him drink very uncomely ... his legs were very weak ... that weakness made him ever leaning on other men's shoulders ... He was the wisest fool in Christendom, wise in small things, but a fool in weighty matters.

James VI of Scotland inherited the Scottish throne in 1567 as a baby when his mother, Mary Queen of Scots, was forced to abdicate, but the country was ruled by nobles until he was older. He was twenty when Mary was executed in 1586. In the late 1580s he began to rule Scotland himself.

Unlike Elizabeth I, James was not interested in grand portraits. This miniature by Nicholas Hilliard was painted soon after he became king of England in 1603.

James was, however, a clever man, already an experienced ruler of Scotland. He saw himself as a peacemaker, and in 1604 he ended England's expensive war with Spain. He also wanted to unite his two kingdoms of Scotland and England, but the English Parliament never agreed.

Empty hopes

With a new king on the throne, both Puritans and Catholics hoped for better times. Puritans wanted more preaching and teaching of the Bible and fewer 'Popish' (Catholic) ceremonies in church services. Catholics longed for an end to the harsh laws of Elizabeth's reign.

51

James was willing to consider the Puritan demands, and, in 1604, held a conference of bishops and leading Puritans at Hampton Court. The two sides agreed only on one point: the need for a new improved English translation of the Bible. *King James's Bible* (also called the Authorised Version) was published in 1611 and became one of the most widely read and important books in the English-speaking world. Many Puritans, however, were disappointed, and resentful because the king had not persuaded the bishops to agree to their demands.

Catholic hopes of greater freedom soon faded. At first James was ready to be more tolerant of them but his Council (led by Robert Cecil, Lord Burghley's son) and Parliament were not. The harsh laws remained, and the peace with Spain seemed to remove any hope of help from Catholics abroad. A small group of Catholic plotters decided there was only one solution – to get rid of both king and Parliament at one blow.

On 5 November 1605 the king would come to open Parliament in the House of Lords. By the night of 4 November, the conspirators had managed to hide thirty-six barrels of gunpowder in a cellar under the Parliament building, apparently without anyone noticing. Guy Fawkes, a soldier from Yorkshire, hid there too, waiting to light the fuse. Just in time, warning reached Robert Cecil and armed guards discovered the gunpowder – and Guy Fawkes. After four days' torture in the Tower, he finally told the truth, and the conspirators were captured and executed.

As the years went by, bonfires celebrated the failure of the Gunpowder Plot every 5 November. English hatred of Catholics increased. Their nickname 'Papist' was used with real venom, and fears of 'Popish' ways in the Church of England became more intense.

This unsigned letter to Lord Monteagle uncovered the plot. It may be from his cousin Thomas Tresham, one of the plotters. It warns him not to go to the House of Lords on 5 November: 'I saye they shall receyve a terrible blowe this parleament' (lines 9 and 10), but makes no mention of an explosion. It may be a forgery. Some historians think that Robert Cecil discovered the plot quite early on and allowed it to continue, to frighten the king and ensure that the laws against Catholics were not changed.

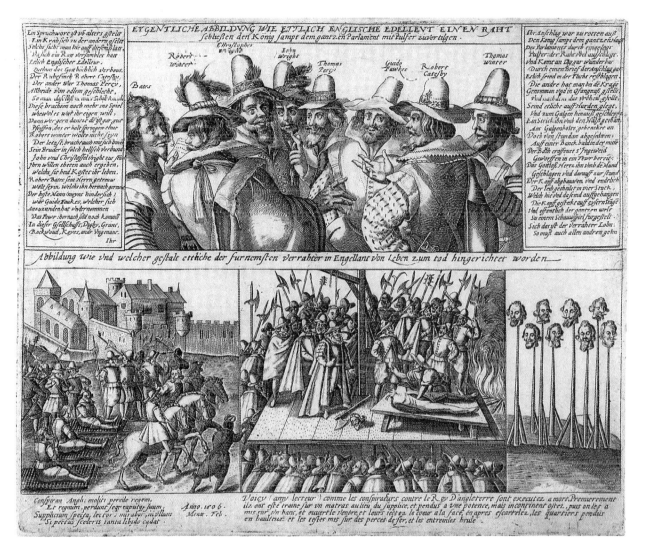

After the discovery of the Gunpowder Plot, printers did well out of selling cheap pictures of the conspirators busy making their evil plans. They also showed their horrible executions in detail.

MPs in Parliament also had hopes of the new king. They expected him to listen to their advice more than Elizabeth had done, especially as he was always short of money. James, on the other hand, liked to emphasize his royal power. In 1610 he told Parliament, 'Kings are not only God's lieutenants upon earth, and sit upon God's throne, but even by God himself they are called gods.' Although people still believed that the king ruled by 'divine right' this was tactless talk from a ruler who wanted Parliament to grant extra taxes.

War with Spain and rising prices had left the Crown with massive debts. Money ran through James's fingers like water. In 1603 alone he spent £20,000 on his coronation and £14,000 on his favourites. He upset MPs by finding new ways of raising money without their consent. Some were disappointed Puritans still hoping for Church reform. In 1614 the 'Addled Parliament' lasted barely six weeks, because MPs refused to grant any money until James listened to their grievances. The king lost patience and dismissed them.

The towne of Pomeiooc and true forme of their howses, couered and enclosed some wth matts, and some wth barcks of trees. All compassed abowt wth smale poles stock thick together in steade of a wall .

An 'Indian' village in Virginia, painted by an Elizabethan explorer, John White, after he visited Virginia in 1596. English settlers there had learned how to grow maize and other crops from the native Americans, or 'Indians' as they called them. In New England too, the settlers learned skills from the 'Indians', and at first lived fairly peacefully alongside them.

New Protestant colonies

Some Puritans decided to leave England and start a new life where they could live and worship as they chose. In 1620 a little ship called *The Mayflower* took 103 of these Pilgrim Fathers, as they came to be called, on a stormy and dangerous journey across the Atlantic Ocean to the coast of North America. In the first terrible winter over half of the settlers died, but the survivors lived to found the colony of Massachusetts.

Although they were still officially ruled by the far-away English king, they lived according to their strict Puritan beliefs. They expected everyone to work hard, wear plain dark clothes, avoid frivolous entertainments and keep Sunday for church-going, without any games or sports. Puritans in England admired their example, and some followed them to found other colonies in 'New England'.

In the north of Ireland also, events led to the creation of a new Protestant colony. On 4 September 1607 a French ship slipped secretly away from the Ulster coast. On board were the earls who had been defeated in 1603, Hugh O'Neill, Earl of Tyrone, and his ally the Earl of

James ordered the settlers to build new towns in Ulster. The City of London merchants took over Derry, and gave it a new English name, Londonderry. This plan of 1619 shows the areas allocated to each trading company.

54

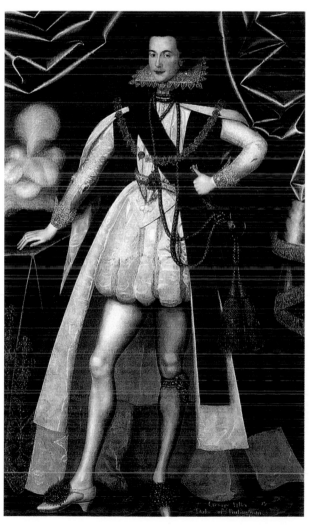

George Villiers, James's favourite, whom he made Duke of Buckingham. This portrait was painted in 1618, soon after his arrival at court. Charming and ruthlessly ambitious, he won the devotion of the old king, who once told his astonished Council, 'Christ had His John, and I have my George.' Buckingham signed his letters to the king 'Your humble slave and dog.' By the 1620s the Duke had beome so powerful that anyone who wanted a position at court had first to win his favour.

Tyrconnel (see page 47). With the 'Flight of the Earls', James now seized the chance to increase his control of Ireland by founding a new colony, this time in Ulster.

Only twelve miles of sea separates Ulster from Scotland. The Catholic Highlanders of Scotland and the Irish had often helped each other in the past, and Highland clansmen had fought alongside O'Neill. Presbyterian Lowland Scots, on the other hand, disapproved of Papists, whether they were Highlanders or Irishmen, and were also hungry for land. James encouraged both the Presbyterian Scots and his English subjects to settle in Ulster.

By 1628, in only twenty years, about 2000 Scots and English had settled in Ulster. The Scots Presbyterians especially were firm in their Protestant faith and full of contempt for the hostile Catholic Irish, whose land they had taken.

The Spanish match

James the peacemaker hoped to act as a bridge between Protestants and Catholics in Europe. He had married his daughter Elizabeth to a German Protestant prince, Frederick of the Palatinate, a small state on the river Rhine. In 1618, against James's advice, Frederick accepted the offer of the crown of Bohemia, a Protestant country which wanted to remain independent of the Catholic emperor. After one winter the emperor's army overran Bohemia, and Elizabeth and Frederick had to flee for their lives. By 1623 the emperor had also conquered the Palatinate, and 'Elizabeth of Bohemia, the Winter Queen', and her family had fled to exile in the Netherlands.

To English MPs the Catholics now seemed triumphant in Europe. They wanted to send an army to help Elizabeth, and start an old-style naval war against Spain, regardless of the cost. James, for once, had a cheaper plan. He would marry his son Charles to the daughter of the Catholic king of Spain, who might persuade the emperor to give back the Palatinate. But the Spaniards showed little interest, and the English hated the idea of a future Spanish queen.

Meanwhile, James's new favourite, the young Duke of Buckingham, was skilfully winning the friendship of James's heir, the lonely and shy Prince Charles. In 1623, in spite of James's disapproval, the two young men slipped off in disguise to woo the Spanish princess in Madrid – an unheard of way to arrange a royal marriage. They soon returned in disgust, without a Spanish queen. James, now a sick old man, reluctantly gave in when Charles and Buckingham, as well as Parliament, demanded war with Spain. Even then Parliament only voted half the money needed. Soon afterwards, in 1625, James died.

A new reign goes wrong

After an uneasy beginning to their marriage, Charles and Henrietta became devoted to each other and he relied on her for advice and support.

This huge portrait (opposite) of Charles, his Queen and their two eldest children Prince Charles (still in skirts) and the baby Mary, is by Anthony Van Dyck. A pupil of the artist Rubens, Van Dyck was one of the best painters in Europe. He arrived in England in 1632 and became Charles's court painter. The royal accounts show that this painting cost £100. It hung at the end of an impressive gallery in Whitehall Palace.

Charles had fine artistic taste and collected pictures from all over Europe. When Rubens visited the English court he said, 'When it comes to fine pictures I have never seen such a large number in one place as in the royal palace'.

Charles I (1625–1649) had been a backward child, late to walk and talk. He was overshadowed by his much-admired elder brother Henry, who, to everyone's deep disappointment, had died suddenly, aged eighteen, in 1612. Charles learned to move with dignity and became a good horseman but he remained reserved and aloof. His loyal follower, the Earl of Clarendon, wrote,

> He kept state to the full, which made his court very orderly … He saw and observed men long before he received any about his person, and did not love strangers, nor very confident men.

The new king was deeply religious, devoted to the Church of England. Like his father, he believed God had given him the right to rule. Charles saw no need to understand how his subjects were feeling, nor to explain any of his actions.

The very unpopular Duke of Buckingham kept his influence over the new king. The king's marriage also did not please his subjects. Instead of a Spanish bride, Charles married a French Catholic princess, Henrietta Maria. The new queen was only fifteen, homesick and rather spoilt. She arrived with her Catholic priests and attendants. She quickly became jealous of Buckingham's influence over the king.

Charles's reign started badly, not only because Buckingham was unpopular but also because the war with Spain was an expensive failure. Then, to try to win popularity, Buckingham unsuccessfully attempted to help some French Protestants who were besieged in the port of La Rochelle by the French king. England, with badly equipped soldiers and a weak navy, was for a time at war with both France and Spain.

Meanwhile, Charles held three stormy Parliaments to try to raise money. MPs refused to co-operate and Charles, who had to find the money somehow, used unpopular methods without Parliament's consent, including a forced loan. When some landowners refused to pay they were imprisoned.

By 1628, Parliament would only agree to grant the money Charles needed if he first accepted a 'Petition of Right'. The king had to promise not to force his subjects to make 'any gift, loan … tax or such like charge without common consent by Act of Parliament', nor was he to imprison them without trial. In return, Parliament at last voted a generous grant of money.

Only six months later Buckingham was murdered. In London crowds celebrated the news of his death and Charles was alone with his grief. Henrietta Maria's influence grew as the king turned to her for comfort and, increasingly, for advice.

King and Parliament continued to disagree, because religion remained a stumbling block. The artistic king loved dignified services, and churches which had altars with a cross and candles, statues and pictures. He appointed churchmen who agreed with him. Puritan MPs saw these changes as Papist and feared Charles was making the Church of England Catholic.

In 1629 Charles had had enough of the arguments over money and religion. He sent orders to the Speaker to dismiss Parliament. As his messenger hammered on the door, the tearful Speaker, who was supposed to control debates, was held down in his chair by a small group of MPs, while the House of Commons passed a declaration condemning the king's policies. Charles imprisoned two of the leaders of the protest in the Tower of London and ordered the MPs to go home.

Eleven years without Parliament

The king now decided he would rule without Parliament, at least for a time. He had to find new ways of raising money and his methods upset people, especially landowners. The worst trouble came from a new tax. English kings had long had the right to tax the ports in order to pay for new ships, but in 1635 Charles made the whole country pay 'Ship Money'. John Hampden, a respected Buckinghamshire landowner, refused to pay. He said the king should not tax his people without Parliament's consent. When he was put on trial five of his twelve judges said Hampden was right. Most people thought Hampden had won the argument, though the king continued collecting Ship Money. He had just enough money to run the country as long as he did not spend on anything extra, such as a war.

Meanwhile the king and his Archbishop of Canterbury, William Laud, made sure that their bishops enforced the changes they wanted in the Church of England. Many people agreed with a Puritan, John Bastwick, who in 1637 wrote a pamphlet attacking bishops:

> They have the keys of Heaven to shut out whom they will. They have the keys of Hell, to thrust in whom they please. They have the keys also of our purses to pick them at their pleasure ... they have the keys of all the prisons in the kingdom ... For the Church is now as full of ceremonies as a dog is full of fleas.

The king and Laud were not Catholics but their actions, and the queen's Catholic priests at court, increased fears that Papists were about to take over the Church and the country. It was Charles's Scottish subjects who first took action against him.

John Bastwick and two other Puritans had their ears cut off and were forced to stand in the pillory in Westminster, surrounded by a sympathetic crowd, as a punishment for writing their pamphlet against bishops. This Puritan cartoon published in 1637 suggests that the hated Archbishop Laud enjoyed eating ears for dinner.

A war the king could not afford

On Sunday 23 July 1637 the bishop in St Giles's Cathedral, Edinburgh used the new Prayer Book. There were shouts from the congregation, then a woman called Jenny Geddes threw a stool at him, and began the violence shown in this picture. In a Glasgow church it was reported that 'some of our honestest women did fall in cursing and scolding' on the minister and 'beat him sore'.

Charles I had neglected his Scottish kingdom. He did not visit it for eight years after he became king. In 1637, without consulting them, he ordered the Scots to use a new Prayer Book which was like the English one. The Presbyterian Scots were furious. All over Scotland people signed the National Covenant, a solemn declaration promising that they would defend their 'Kirk' (Church). The Scots also had a good army, and as the king refused to give in, they decided to fight.

Now Charles was faced with a war he could not afford, as well as a tax strike among his English and Welsh subjects. By 1640 almost no money was being collected from either the Welsh or English counties, and when a battle looked likely in Scotland, Charles's unpaid, badly equipped English soldiers ran away. To raise more money, the king summoned Parliament in April 1640. MPs refused him a penny until he changed his policies, so after three weeks Charles dismissed this 'Short Parliament'.

The Scots marched over the border, occupied Newcastle and demanded £850 a day from the king to pay their soldiers. With no money and a defeated raggle-taggle army, Charles was forced to call another Parliament. The Scots and Charles's opponents in England, who were secretly in touch with each other, now knew that the king would have to agree to Parliament's demands.

The Arch-Prelate of St Andrewes in Scotland reading the new Service-booke in his pontificalibus assaulted by men & women, with Crickett stooles sticks and stones.

The Long Parliament

The Earl of Strafford was the king's most loyal and able minister. This is a copy of a painting done by Charles's court painter Van Dyck in 1636.

Strafford had ruled Ireland for the king from 1633, and his enemies feared he had built up an army there to help Charles in England. He was recalled by Charles in 1639 to help him with the Scots. Strafford had few friends, mainly because of his 'sour and haughty temper'.

When Parliament condemned him to death he told Charles to agree. He wrote, 'to set your Majesty's conscience at liberty, I do most humbly beseech your Majesty (for prevention of evils which may happen at your refusal) to pass this Bill'. His execution took place on Tower Hill, London, before a huge crowd.

In November 1640, the 'Long Parliament' met. It is called 'Long' because it was not dismissed officially by a king for twenty years. The leader of the House of Commons was John Pym, a shrewd, clever Puritan lawyer and a friend of John Hampden. Pym attacked the king's advisers and whipped up feeling against Catholics. He wanted to ensure that the king could never again rule without Parliament, and almost all MPs agreed with him.

Parliament was determined to remove the king's two most important ministers, Archbishop Laud and the Earl of Strafford, and sent them to the Tower. Laud was left to rot in prison (he was later executed in 1645) but Strafford was condemned to death by Act of Parliament. When Charles refused to agree to his execution, a violent mob outside Whitehall Palace

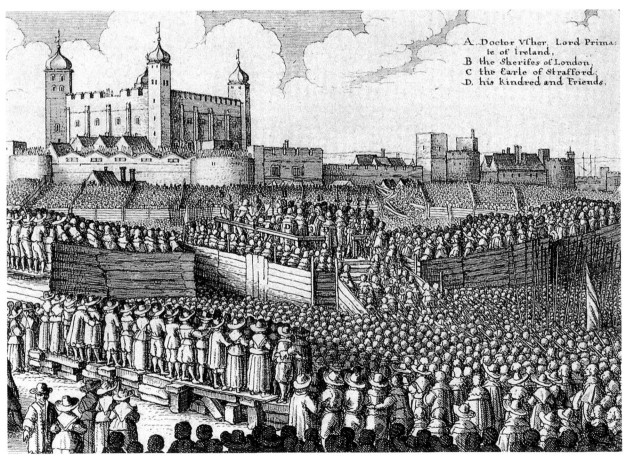

A. Doctor Vsher, Lord Primate of Ireland,
B the Sherifes of London,
C the Earle of Strafford,
D. his kindred and friends.

threatened the unpopular queen and the king gave in. In May 1641 Strafford was beheaded, with London crowds shouting in glee, 'his head is off!' Charles never forgave himself for deserting his minister.

By the summer of 1641, Parliament had abolished Ship Money and the other ways in which the king had raised money without their consent. A new law said Parliament must meet every three years, even if the king did not agree. Some Puritan MPs wanted to abolish bishops, but others feared that things were changing too fast. Crowds of Londoners were out on the streets violently demonstrating their support for Pym and the Puritans, and there were reports of trouble in the countryside. Those with land and position were afraid of losing control.

Driuinge Men Women & children by hund: reds vpon Briges & casting them into Riuers, who drowned not were killed with poles & shot with muskets.

In October 1641 horrifying tales of murdered and tortured Protestants filled English news-sheets. At the bridge of Portadown in Ulster, Catholic rebels drove Protestants into the river below and murdered most of them in the water.

This terrible event became even worse when it was reported in an English news-sheet that the massacre had happened not just once, but all over Ireland.

In October 1641, amid all this confusion, news of a rebellion in Ireland reached London. Catholics in Ulster had risen against the Protestant settlers, and Pym made the most of the increasing fears of Catholic plots. He put forward a law to give Parliament, not the king, control of the army needed to crush the Irish. This would make Charles powerless. Pym also forced through the Grand Remonstrance, a long list of objections to Charles's actions (many of them by now dealt with). It was passed with violent arguments, by only eleven votes, as support for the king grew among moderate MPs. The House of Commons, like the nation, was split down the middle.

Urged on by the queen, and believing there was a plot against him, Charles took action. On 4 January 1642 he set out with 300 soldiers from Whitehall Palace to arrest Pym, Hampden and three other MPs in the House of Commons. Warning reached Pym just in time, and the five members escaped by boat to the City of London, where they were safe among the apprentices and shopkeepers who supported them so strongly.

Charles walked into the silent House of Commons and demanded to know where the five members were. The Speaker, William Lenthall, knelt respectfully and replied:

May it please Your Majesty, I have neither eyes to see nor tongue to speak in this place, but as this House is pleased to direct me, whose servant I am here.

The king realized he had been outwitted. 'I see the birds have flown', he said. As he left, MPs shouted 'Privilege! Privilege!' at him, reminding him fiercely of their right not to be arrested in Parliament. Charles had tried force and it had failed. London was in an uproar, and it was too dangerous for him to stay. He travelled north to raise an army. The five members returned to Westminster in triumph, and their supporters also began to raise troops. If Charles wanted to return to his capital, he would have to fight for it.

Armies on the march

The king had one clear aim – to win back his capital, London. He also needed to win the war quickly, before his money ran out and Parliament's advantages over supplies had time to take effect.

As Charles I began to lead the troops he had raised towards London from the west midlands, Parliament's army set out from London to stop him. It was commanded by the Earl of Essex, the son of Elizabeth I's executed favourite, a hard-working, cautious man who had the depressing habit of going into battle with his coffin prepared.

On 23 October 1642 the two armies blundered into each other at Edgehill in Warwickshire. Prince Rupert's cavalry charged, and almost broke up the Roundhead army, but he could not prevent his Cavaliers from sweeping off the battlefield to loot a nearby village. The rest of the battle was a tough fight on foot, which nobody won, and which left unknown numbers dead or dying in the cold October night.

Then the king and Rupert marched on to London, but their exhausted troops failed to get past the London trainbands (local troops paid for and equipped by the citizens) at Turnham Green outside the city. This was the nearest the Royalists ever came to London, and from now on it was clear they would not win the war quickly.

Meanwhile, the king had decided to make his headquarters at Oxford. As the war spread, fighting affected many areas. In 1643 the Royalists again failed to reach London, but they had some successes. Prince Rupert caught John Hampden's troops at Chalgrove, east of Oxford, and Hampden was mortally wounded. His death, and John Pym's from cancer, were both serious losses for Parliament. Rupert also captured the important port of Bristol. But the king failed to take nearby Gloucester, so Roundhead troops based there continued to disrupt essential Royalist supply routes from south Wales.

Prince Rupert, the king's nephew, was a tough and daring cavalry leader who inspired his men, although he often upset older commanders on his own side. Roundheads soon began to fear they could not defeat him, and that his big white hunting poodle called Boye, the 'devil dog poodle', bewitched them.

A musket was heavy, and it took about one minute and twenty different actions to load it – a long time if a cavalry charge was thundering down.

The war brought new and often terrible experiences to many people. In all wars before the twentieth century, more soldiers died from disease than from battle wounds, although a soldier was lucky if he recovered from those. In the crowded dirty conditions in which soldiers lived, killer diseases like typhus (called camp fever) spread rapidly and local people caught them. In crowded wartime Oxford there were two bad epidemics, in 1643 and 1644. About one fifth of the population died in the war years.

Villagers who lived in areas crossed by both armies often had to pay taxes to both sides, and provide them with corn, cattle and horses. Women kept the household going when their menfolk were away, and some were involved in the fighting. The Parliamentarian Lady Brilliana Harley defended her house, Brampton Bryan Castle, and died during the siege.

Women often had good reason to dislike both sides. The village women of Kilsby in Northamptonshire took matters into their own hands after their menfolk had attacked some of the Royalist garrison from Banbury. In return, the Royalists plundered the village and took away the men and (perhaps worse still) all the cattle to Banbury. The women cursed the plundering soldiers, and marched to Banbury. They forced their men to agree to pay the taxes they owed, and then 'men, women and cattle returned to the place whence they came', and seem to have been left in peace.

A cartoon makes fun of a soldier laden with stolen loot, although people who lost household and farm equipment did not find it amusing.

As the war continued, local people in the Welsh borders and the south-west banded together to attack both sides. These 'Clubmen' only had clubs, pitchforks or scythes to use as weapons, so they achieved little except to show their feelings about the way in which the war was ruining their lives.

Stubble to our swords

By the summer of 1644, Parliament was gaining the advantage. The Scots agreed to invade England again. In return, Parliament promised that a Presbyterian Kirk would be set up in England.

Parliament's own armies were changing. A new military leader had appeared, in addition to Sir Thomas Fairfax. Oliver Cromwell was a Puritan MP from Huntingdon. Disappointed by the performance of the Roundhead troops at Edgehill, he went home to train his own cavalry. He picked his men carefully, especially the officers. When he was criticized for choosing officers who were not all gentlemen, he said,

I had rather have a plain russet-coated captain that knows what he fights for and loves what he knows, than what you call a gentleman and is nothing else … If you choose godly honest men to be captains of horse, honest men will follow them.

This miniature portrait of Oliver Cromwell was painted by Samuel Cooper after the war in 1656. Cromwell had strong, heavy features, and he did not like being flattered. He once told an artist who painted his portrait that he would not pay him if his picture did not show all 'these ruffnesses, pimples and warts as you see me'. Unlike some Puritans, Cromwell enjoyed art and music.

He trained his strictly disciplined troops to charge at a fast trot instead of a gallop, so that they did not become uncontrolled as Rupert's horsemen did. He cared for his men and did his best to see they were paid regularly. He never once lost a battle.

Prince Rupert, who recognized a good soldier when he saw one, gave Cromwell the nickname 'old Ironsides', and the name spread to his troops. The Ironsides and the Scots helped to bring about the first serious Royalist defeat at Marston Moor, near York, in 1644. Cromwell wrote afterwards, 'God made them as stubble to our swords.' The king had now lost the north of England, but he still controlled most of Wales and the south-west.

The Roundhead leaders disagreed about what to do next. The Earl of Manchester, a cautious commander like Essex, had doubts about continuing the war and told Cromwell, 'If we beat the King ninety and nine times, yet he is King still, but if the King beat us once, we shall all be hanged'. Cromwell angrily replied, 'My Lord if this be so, why did we take up arms at first? This is against fighting ever hereafter.'

In the end, Parliament listened to Cromwell. The unsuccessful commanders Essex and Manchester lost their jobs. Parliament now set up a 'New Model Army', the first national army, commanded by General Fairfax with Cromwell second in command.

At first the Cavaliers scoffed at the 'New Noddle Army', but not for long. In June 1645 the New Model Army won the last great battle of the war which took place at Naseby, near Leicester. Dazed by defeat, the king had no money to raise another army, although the war dragged on until 1646. The Royalists lost the south-west, and Oxford was besieged. Finally the king gave himself up to the Scots, and Oxford surrendered two months later without a battle.

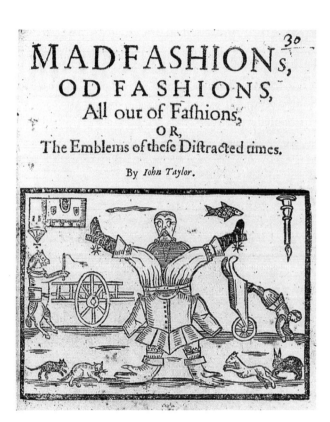

This picture was on the title page of a pamphlet called The World Turned Upside Down, *printed in 1649, when many people felt everything was topsy-turvy. A man walks on his hands, a mouse chases a cat, a rabbit chases a dog ... and a great deal more.*

The world turned upside down 1646–1649

'You have now done your work, boys, you may go play, unless you fall out amongst yourselves,' said an old Royalist officer, Sir Jacob Astley, to his Roundhead captors as fighting ended in 1646. The victorious Roundhead side was indeed deeply divided.

The Scots soon handed the king over to Parliament, but they still wanted their reward for their part in victory – a Scots Presbyterian Church in England. Parliament resented Scots interference but many MPs also feared the power of their victorious and expensive Army, and wanted to send the soldiers home.

Soldiers in the Army shared Cromwell's feelings before Naseby, when he said, 'I could not ... but smile out to God in praises, in assurance of victory ... and God did it.' They wanted to profit from the victory which they and God had won. Some of them were 'Levellers', who were also strong in London. Levellers believed, as one of their leaders described it,

The poorest he that is in England hath a life to live, as the greatest he; ... every man that is to live under a government ought first by his own consent to put himself under that government.

Although Cromwell and the Army officers agreed with some Leveller ideas, such as cheap and fair law courts, they (and all landowners) thought it a dangerous idea that 'the poorest he' should have a vote, and they feared the Levellers would split the Army. To Cromwell, the Army's swords were the only guarantee of creating a peaceful government but, to achieve that, an even more pressing problem than the Levellers had to be solved.

The Army had, as well as their swords, a trump card – the king, who had been kidnapped from Parliament and was being kept at Hampton Court. Charles was isolated, but serenely confident that God would restore his royal power as his enemies fell out. He refused a peace offer from the Army, escaped to the Isle of Wight and was recaptured. While discussing peace with Parliament he made a secret deal with the Scots, who now hoped that if they won him back his kingdom, they would be in control. A brief and bloody second civil war broke out; Cromwell quickly defeated the Royalists and Scots.

The Army leaders were furious at the king's double dealing. They had already decided that 'Charles Stuart, that man of blood' should be publicly tried for treason against his people. Many MPs were horrified, and still wanted to make peace with the king. On a cold December morning in 1648, soldiers prevented these MPs from entering the House of Commons. Only about a third of the Long Parliament now remained, nicknamed the 'Rump'. It was ready, the Army hoped, to do the soldiers' bidding. After a five-day trial in Westminster Hall, the king was found guilty and sentenced to death by public execution.

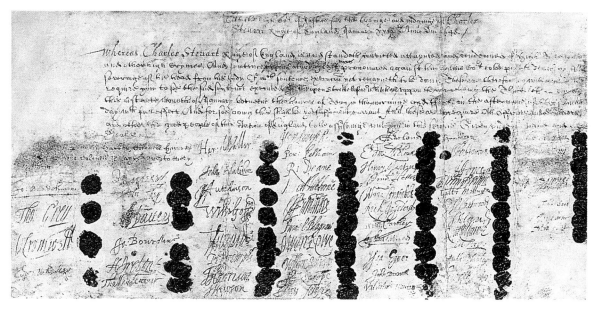

The army leaders chose 135 people to be judges at the king's trial, but many were too frightened, or too disapproving, to turn up. Only 59 dared to sign this death warrant which ordered the king's execution. One of them defiantly declared, when facing execution eleven years later for murdering the king, that 'it was not a thing done in a corner'.

The day of Charles I's execution, 30 January 1649, was bitterly cold. The king put on two shirts so that he would not shiver, and seem afraid. 'Death is not terrible to me,' he said. The scaffold in front of his beautiful Banqueting House in Whitehall was surrounded by huge, silent crowds, with soldiers everywhere. The king's last words made it clear he still believed he was in the right:

> All the world knows I never did begin a war with the two Houses of Parliament … They began these unhappy troubles, not I … For the people … I must tell you that their liberty and their freedom consists in having of government … It is not for having a share in government … A subject and a sovereign are clean different things …

The execution of Charles I shocked the whole of Europe. The foreign artist who painted this scene was almost certainly not an eyewitness, but he knew about the crowds. The soldiers are cheering, but others are very upset. Many people, who had not liked the way Charles ruled, admired the way he died.

Before the axe fell, the king said one more word, 'Remember'. A seventeen-year-old boy who watched the execution said, 'there was such a groan by the thousands then present, as I never heard before, and desire I may never hear again.'

The Rump Parliament declared England to be a 'Commonwealth'. They abolished the monarchy and the House of Lords. The Church of England had already been abolished in 1644 by the Long Parliament and people were ordered to use the Scots prayerbook.

Meanwhile Cromwell and the Army were fully occupied, guarding the Commonwealth from attack. First Cromwell crushed the Levellers, to keep his Army united. Then he set out to safeguard England's two 'back doors': Ireland and Scotland.

Papist and Presbyterian enemies

In Ireland some Royalist troops still held out, backed by the Catholic Irish. Cromwell conducted his harshest campaign there. After he had captured the town of Drogheda he reported to Parliament,

> I forbade them to spare any that were in arms in the town, and I think that night they put to the sword about 2000 men ... When they submitted, their officers were knocked on the head, and every tenth man of the soldiers killed; and the rest shipped for Barbados ... I am persuaded that this is a righteous judgment of God upon these barbarous wretches ... and that it will tend to prevent effusion [shedding] of blood for the future.

It took Cromwell almost a year to conquer Ireland. The war brought plague and famine. Catholic services were forbidden and priests were executed, or imprisoned. The Irish lost yet more land to Cromwell's officers and to English people who had given money to pay for the Irish war.

The Scots also threatened the new Commonwealth. They resented the army leaders' decision to execute Charles I without their consent, for he was king of Scotland as well as England. They made a deal with the young Charles II, who came to Scotland from exile in the Dutch Republic. Cromwell marched north and, although heavily outnumbered, defeated the Scots at Dunbar on 3 September 1650. The next year, Charles II invaded England with a Scots army. Cromwell caught them at Worcester, once again on 3 September, and won his last great victory, his 'crowning mercy' as he called it.

Scotland became a defeated country, occupied by an English army, although Cromwell did not treat the Protestant Scots as harshly as the Catholic Irish, and they did not lose their land. Both Ireland and Scotland were unwillingly part of a united Britain under Cromwell.

Charles II was on the run for six weeks after his defeat at Worcester. A reward of £1000 was offered for 'a tall young man two yards high, with hair deep brown to black', but no one betrayed him. Here he hides in an oak tree while Roundhead soldiers search for him. After he won back his crown in 1660, pictures like this of his adventures were very popular, and many inns were called 'The Royal Oak.'

The Protector's sword rule 1653–1658

After Cromwell returned from his conquests, he found that MPs in the Rump Parliament were clinging to power. He also disliked the trading war they were waging against Dutch Protestants. In April 1653 he stormed into the House of Commons in disgust, and dismissed the Rump. He ordered a new Parliament to be chosen from local Puritan churches, but to his great disappointment the 'Rule of the Saints' achieved little, and soon gave back their power to the Army leaders.

The Army now drew up a new plan. In December 1653 Cromwell became Lord Protector, ruling with Parliament. But a new Parliament

A cartoon of Cromwell, by his enemies, shows him as a villain and cruel dictator. He stands on the slippery mouth of Hell as he orders his followers to cut down the Tree of Great Britain, which bears the crown, Parliament's laws, Magna Carta and the Bible. The pigs are the ordinary, ignorant people he is leading astray.

(below) Cromwell by his supporters, shown as the Lord Protector, holding the Bible. The pillars represent his power, and the dove of peace flies above his head. He crushes war under his feet, and below him his people live peaceful, prosperous lives, ploughing, caring for their sheep and gathering their crops.

still full of landowners distrusted Cromwell's power, and resented the huge cost of the Army.

In 1656, after a Royalist rising, Cromwell went back to 'sword rule'. He appointed eleven Major-Generals, who, pushing aside the local landowners, each ran an area of the country. They collected heavy taxes. Some were strict Puritans and closed alehouses, and stopped horse-racing. Parliament had already closed London's theatres and forbidden people to celebrate Christmas. People did not forget what it was like to be ruled by soldiers.

Then Parliament offered Cromwell the crown, probably to try to go back to the old ways. We do not know if Cromwell really wanted to be 'King Oliver', but most of his beloved Army hated the idea. In the end he refused.

The country remained peaceful. Although Cromwell had treated Irish Catholics harshly, he did not persecute people for their religion in England. He allowed Jews to live and work in Britain for the first time since 1290. He tried, unsuccessfully, to stop Parliament punishing a Quaker, James Nayler, who rode into Bristol on a donkey as if he was Jesus riding into Jerusalem. Nayler was probably mentally ill, but Quakers

Cromwell's head. His corpse was treated like that of a king, and buried in Westminster Abbey. When Charles II became king, it was dug up, and the head cut off and stuck up on the gallows at Tyburn. Later it became part of a peepshow at a fair. This photograph was taken before the head was finally buried in 1960 at Sidney Sussex College, Cambridge, where Cromwell was a student.

(or the Society of Friends) were often persecuted, because their ideas seemed dangerous. The Quakers were founded in the early 1650s by a weaver called George Fox. They did not have organized church services,but waited for the spirit of God to inspire them, often quaking and shaking with emotion. They allowed women to preach and refused to swear oaths, even in a law court. Most shocking of all, they treated rich and poor as equals.

Abroad, Cromwell won respect, in spite of the horror European rulers had felt for the 'king-murderers' in 1649. He ended the Dutch war, and made trade treaties with Denmark and Portugal. War with Spain led to the capture of Jamaica in 1655, and his army defeated the Spaniards at the 'Battle of the Dunes' and won Dunkirk, which gave England a base on Europe's mainland once again. The costs of war were enormous, but even the Royalist Clarendon admitted that Cromwell's 'greatness at home was but a shadow of the glory he had abroad.'

Yet by 1658 Cromwell was a sad old man. His favourite daughter died, and he fell ill. He died just after a great storm, on 3 September, the same date as his earlier victories at Dunbar and Worcester. His secretary wrote, 'There is not a dog wags its tongue, so great a calm we are in.'

Oliver's eldest son, Richard Cromwell, became Protector for a few months, but he won little respect and the country slid into chaos. Then, late in 1659 General Monck, Cromwell's commander in Scotland, marched south with his army. In 1660, with Monck's backing, a newly elected Parliament invited Charles II (1660–1685) to return to his kingdom.

CHAPTER 7

A king again

❖

On New Year's Day 1660 a young Londoner called Samuel Pepys began to write a diary. That year he had a new job at the Navy Office, organizing supplies and pay, and he sometimes also went to court. His diary describes his everyday life too. On 16 January 1660, after an evening spent drinking and singing with friends, he went home late,

> where I found my wife and maid a-washing. I sat up till the bellman came by with his bell, just under my window, as I was writing of this very line, and cried, 'Past one of the clock, and a cold, frosty, windy morning.' I then went to bed and left my wife and the maid a-washing still.

Pepys wrote his diary in shorthand. It begins: 'Blessed be God, at the end of last year, I was in very good health … I lived in Axe Yard, having my wife and servant Jane, and no more in family but us three.' When he had his portrait painted in 1666 (below), he wrote: 'I sit to have it full of shadows, and do almost break my neck looking over my shoulder to make the posture for him [the artist John Hayls] to work by'.

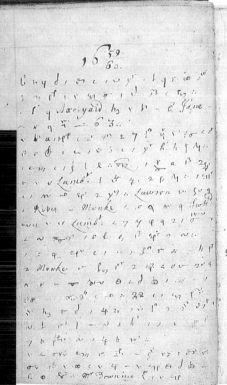

Charles II rides in procession to his coronation. Pepys got up at 4 a.m. to get a seat in Westminster Abbey, but when the crown was placed on the king's head 'to my very great grief I and most in the Abbey could not see.' But as for the whole day, Pepys was 'sure never to see the like again in this world.'

The year 1660 proved to be an exciting one. John Evelyn, a Surrey landowner who also kept a diary, watched King Charles II's return to London on 29 May:

With a triumph of above 20,000 horse and foot, brandishing their swords and shouting with inexpressible joy; the ways strewed with flowers, the bells ringing, the streets hung with tapestry, fountains running wine ... I stood in the Strand, and beheld it, and blessed God.

The watching crowds rejoiced because they were tired of 'sword rule', the heavy taxes the army had brought, and Puritan strictness, which they connected with war and rebellion. Since Catholics were still feared as dangerous plotters and supporters of enemies abroad, many people now welcomed back the Church of England as a safe 'middle way'.

Charles II was clever enough to realize how most of his subjects were feeling, and had no wish, 'to go on his travels again.' The thirty-year-old king was witty and charming, but eleven hard years of exile had taught him to trust no one. He avoided work if he could – 'the ruin of his reign was his giving himself up to a mad range of pleasures', observed the disapproving Scots Bishop Burnet.

Charles's pleasures included the theatre, gambling and horse-racing. His court was a worldly, extravagant place, and there was no secret about his many mistresses, nor the children (probably seventeen) he had by them. He did not change his ways when, in 1662, he married a shy Catholic princess from Portugal, Catherine of Braganza.

The king knew he must work with the ruling classes in Parliament, if he was to keep his throne. The old problem of money remained. The taxes voted by Parliament did not bring in the £1,200,000 they had promised. Although Catherine of Braganza brought a useful dowry, the extravagant Charles was soon in debt.

Memories of Cromwell's 'sword rule' made Parliament determined not to have a permanent army. The New Model Army was sent home at last, although Charles was allowed to keep the Coldstream Guards, who still protect the sovereign today.

Charles also knew he must support the Church of England. He may have been a Catholic at heart, but he realized he would lose his throne if he ever admitted it. He wanted to allow all his subjects to worship freely, but the enthusiastic MPs in the 'Cavalier Parliament' elected in 1661 had different ideas.

New laws made the restored Church of England more powerful than it had ever been. Over 1000 Puritan clergy lost their jobs, all Puritan services were forbidden and no Puritan could preach within five miles of towns which sent MPs to Parliament. Secret Puritan groups still met in other, newer towns, and in the countryside. They were called Dissenters, or Nonconformists, and the name Puritan died out. As the years passed it was the Church of England which suffered most. It became the church of the ruling classes, and its clergy were often cut off from ordinary people.

In Wales, men like the Quaker Thomas Wynne suffered under the new laws. In 1682, after six years in prison, he led a group of Welsh Quakers to the new Quaker colony of Pennsylvania in America. In spite of their persecution, Dissenters were winning growing support in Wales.

In these difficult years the poet John Milton, who had worked for Cromwell, was in disgrace. Yet although he was blind and often ill, Milton completed his great masterpiece, the story poem *Paradise Lost*, which was published in 1667.

Cromwell's 'glory abroad' soon disappeared with the changing situation in Europe. France's young ruler, Louis XIV, was determined to be the greatest monarch in Europe. As he built his huge palace at

(right) Charles II's queen, Catherine of Braganza, arrived at the worldly English court looking prim and old-fashioned in her stiff, high-necked dress with its hooped skirt. She soon began to dress fashionably, and in 1663 Pepys wrote 'The Queen begins to be brisk and play like other ladies.'

(far right) The beautiful, grasping and fashionable Barbara Castlemaine, painted by the court artist Peter Lely. She was the king's favourite mistress at the time of his marriage. Catherine soon learned that she had to ignore her husband's unfaithfulness, and his children by other women. She had none of her own.

Versailles, he also embarked on a series of wars to expand France's frontiers north into the Netherlands and east into the German states. Charles II admired his rich and powerful cousin, the 'Sun King'. But his subjects feared the rising power of Catholic France, which now seemed more dangerous than the old enemy, Spain.

The Protestant Dutch Republic had broken free from Spain in 1609, and had grown rich through trade. Trading rivalry led to three wars with England between 1652 and 1674. By the 1670s Louis XIV was threatening the Dutch, and they needed English friendship. Many English people were also by this time less enthusiastic about fighting Dutch Protestants, when Catholic France was growing so strong.

England had another link with the Dutch: their ruler was William of Orange, a nephew of Charles II. He was determined to stand up to Louis XIV and defend his small country against French aggression.

John Bunyan, a poor tinker from Bedford who became a famous preacher, was imprisoned for being an active Nonconformist. This is the first page of his famous book Pilgrim's Progress, *written in prison and published in 1678. Bunyan dreams of the story he wrote, in which the hero Christian sets out on a long and dangerous journey from the City of Destruction to the Celestial City in Heaven.*

In 1667 panic spread when the Dutch sailed right into the main naval dockyard in Kent, burning several ships and capturing the pride of the navy, the battleship Royal Charles, *shown in the centre of this picture. Pepys was desperately overworked at the Navy Office, and in such 'frights and fear' that he sent his money and other valuables out of London.*

Fears of ruin

The joyful mood of 1660 soon faded. Royalists expected large rewards for their earlier loyalty but were mostly disappointed. Pepys, although he enjoyed watching grand court occasions, and admired the ladies there, was in despair in 1666 about 'the sad, vicious and negligent Court, and all sober men fearful of the ruin of the whole kingdom.'

London was also hit by two terrible disasters. First, in the hot summer of 1665, the dreaded bubonic plague returned. Pepys stayed in plague-stricken London, although the court and most wealthy citizens fled, including many doctors:

7 June It being the hottest day that ever I felt in my life ... this day much against my will, I did in Drury Lane see two or three houses marked with a red cross upon the doors, and 'Lord have mercy upon us' writ there – which was a sad sight to me ... I was forced to buy some roll-tobacco to smell and chaw – which took away the apprehension ...

London officials recorded over 68,000 deaths from plague in 1665. The total was probably higher, and the plague spread to other places.

Early on 2 September 1666 a baker's oven in Pudding Lane, in the heart of London, caught fire and, fanned by a strong wind, the flames spread rapidly. The great Fire of London burned for four terrible days. St Paul's Cathedral and eighty-seven other churches were in ruins. About 13,000 houses were burned, and perhaps 100,000 people made homeless. Although Pepys and many others knew how the fire had started, inevitably people blamed the Catholics.

The future also seemed uncertain. Charles II and Catherine had no children. The heir to the throne was Charles's brother James, Duke of York, a devout Catholic. James never understood the panic which his religion caused his future subjects, who were terrified he would burn Protestants and destroy Parliament. He probably had no intention of doing either, but he held the unrealistic belief that once English people understood the Catholic faith, they would all join the 'true Church'.

James became even more unpopular after his second marriage in 1673, to a young Catholic princess from the Italian state of Modena, Mary Beatrice, whose family was backed by Louis XIV. The English did not want a future queen who was another Papist, and connected with the feared French.

The view that Pepys saw of the Fire of London at night, with St Paul's Cathedral burning in the centre, as he watched from across the river, with the wind blowing 'a shower of firedrops' in his face – 'A most horrid malicious bloody flame ... We saw the fire as only one entire arch of fire ... above a mile long. It made me weep to see it. The churches, houses and all on fire and flaming at once, and a horrid noise the flames made, and the cracking of houses at their ruin.'

Whigs and Tories

By 1678 those who opposed James were so well organized that historians often call them the first political party – the Whigs. At first 'Whig' was a rude nickname for them, meaning a violent Scots rebel, but it stuck. The Whigs, supported by the anti-Catholic London crowds, had a simple aim: to stop James becoming king by persuading Parliament to pass an 'Exclusion Bill', to exclude him from inheriting the throne.

In 1678 the Whigs were greatly helped by an extraordinary scare that there was a terrible 'Popish Plot', backed by the Pope and the French, to kill Charles and make James king. Innocent Catholics were hunted down, and eighteen priests were executed. Parliament had by now also passed two 'Test Acts', which prevented Catholics from being MPs, holding positions on town councils, or in the army and navy. Their situation was now worse than it had ever been.

In this hysterical atmosphere, the Whigs nearly pushed their Exclusion Bill through Parliament. However, Charles II was determined to protect his brother's right to the throne. The Whigs rudely called his supporters 'Tories', a name for Irish robbers who lurked in bogs and mugged travellers. Their nickname has survived, although its old meaning is long forgotten.

The Tories still believed that kings ruled by God's will, so they must accept James, but as firm supporters of the Church of England, they did not welcome a Catholic king any more than the Whigs. The realistic Charles, however, had insisted that James's daughters by his first marriage, Mary and Anne, were brought up in the Church of England. Mary, the heir, was married to Protestant William of Orange. The elderly James's second marriage had produced no children, so Tories thought the future was safe.

As people became more frightened of another civil war than of imaginary Popish plots, the Tories won support. Charles held a Parliament in Oxford in 1681, away from Whig London. Trade had improved his income and, as Louis XIV had secretly sent him money as well, he did not need Parliament to raise funds. He quickly dissolved it, and did not call it again during his lifetime. The Whigs were defeated.

In February 1685 Charles had a stroke while shaving. As the king lay dying, James smuggled in a priest and Charles accepted the Catholic faith. This is probably the best clue we have to Charles's real beliefs.

Charles in his later years, painted in 1680 by Edward Hawker. He began to wear a wig in 1666 because, Pepys said, he was going 'mighty grey'. The fashion caught on for men and lasted for over a century.

A king goes on his travels

The Queen is brought to bed
of a Boy

Reported so

A story intended to shock people: this picture on a playing card was intended to encourage people to believe stories that the queen's son had been born dead and another baby (a miller's son) smuggled into her bed. The child would therefore, of course, have no right to become the next king.

Charles II had once said he was afraid that when his brother became king he would 'be obliged to travel again'. When he came to the throne James II (1685–1688) soon lost any support he might have won if he had acted more tactfully.

After an unsuccessful rebellion in the south-west by Charles II's illegitimate son, the Duke of Monmouth, James decided to keep an army just outside London. His subjects found this threatening, especially as, in spite of Parliament's Test Act, he had appointed several Irish Catholic officers.

The Catholic Mass was now celebrated openly in London churches and in the great cathedrals, such as Durham. In January 1687 the horrified John Evelyn watched 'a world of mysterious ceremony' at the king's new chapel, 'not believing I should ever have lived to see such things in the King of England's palace, after it had pleased God to enlighten this nation.'

James tried to win over Dissenters by declaring that they, as well as Catholics, could worship freely in spite of Parliament's laws, but most of them continued to distrust this Papist king. When the Archbishop of Canterbury and six other bishops refused to accept James's action, the king sent them to the Tower of London. They were put on trial but, to James's fury, found not guilty. Excited Londoners, who were not usually fond of bishops, cheered as they walked free.

Meanwhile, in June 1688, a healthy son, James Edward, was born at last to James's queen. The baby would be brought up a Catholic, and become the next monarch instead of Protestant Mary, wife of William of Orange. The future was no longer safe. Seven leading Whigs and Tories wrote secretly to William of Orange, offering to support him if he brought an army over to England.

In the Netherlands William was expecting an attack from Louis XIV. He wanted the English on his side, but he risked a great deal if he took an army to England, leaving his own country undefended. It was autumn and his fleet might face dangerous storms as it sailed to England, and the prevailing wind anyway blew in the wrong direction.

Two pieces of luck solved William's problems. Instead of attacking the Dutch, Louis XIV invaded the German state of the Palatinate. The French king thought (wrongly) that if William took his army to England he would be kept there by a long war. Louis planned to invade the undefended Netherlands at that point.

Then, unusually for November, the wind changed. This 'Protestant wind', as it was later called, blew from the north-east, speeding William's ships down the Channel. He landed at Torbay in Devon on 5 November 1688, far from any opposition. James's army melted away as he went into a frozen panic, and leading landowners and MPs joined William. The queen fled to France with her baby son, and James soon followed them. William and his troops reached London without a fight.

No-one knew quite what to do next. Mary, James's daughter, and William's wife, had a better right to rule than William, but she dutifully backed her husband when he refused to be 'his wife's gentleman lackey [servant]'. Finally Parliament agreed that William III (1689–1702) and Mary II (1689–1694) should rule together as joint and equal monarchs.

The powerful landowners in Parliament set out limits on royal power in a Bill of Rights of 1689. No monarch could set aside laws made by Parliament. The monarch must not be a Catholic, nor marry a Catholic.

Royal power was limited in other ways. England was now involved in William's struggle with France, and enormous sums of money were regularly needed for war. Parliament paid for the army and the navy separately from other royal expenses, and William was forced to rely on it to meet the costs of war. Since 1689, Parliament has met every year.

A shortage of royal children also increased Parliament's influence. William and Mary had no children. After William's death in 1702, Mary's sister Anne (1702–1714) became the next queen. All of her seventeen children died young. In 1701 Parliament decided they should choose who should rule next. It had to be a Protestant. They chose a great-grandson of James I, George, the Protestant ruler of the German state of Hanover. When Anne died in 1714 he became George I (1714–1727), the first Hanoverian king of England.

A few Tories continued to support James II and his son. These 'Jacobites' (from *Jacobus*, the Latin name for James) had little influence. The changes of 1688–1689 came to be called 'The Glorious Revolution'. English landowners in Parliament thought it 'glorious' for two reasons. There were no battles or executions, at least in England, and from that time their power increased and royal power declined.

William and Mary ride in state to the Banqueting House to accept their joint crowns. John Evelyn described William as 'stately, serious and reserved'. He was never popular in England, and always preferred his Dutch advisers. Mary was charming and outgoing. In 1688 she had to make a difficult choice between supporting her husband or her father. She backed William with devotion, and seems to have been content to be a submissive wife.

England's back doors

In Wales William was never popular, but many Welsh people feared a possible Catholic attack from the nearby coasts of Ireland. Their new rulers offered the best protection. In rich Welsh households after 1660, clothes, food and manners became more English, and it was no longer fashionable to employ Welsh poets. Nevertheless, the Welsh language did not die. The growing numbers of Dissenters listened to Welsh preachers, and in parish churches people heard the Welsh Prayer Book every Sunday.

James II's army besieging Derry, protected in the foreground by earthworks covered in wicker. Beyond the city is the boom across the harbour, and the desperately-needed English supply ships lurk on the horizon. The townspeople survived by eating dogs, mice, rats, candle ends and leather until the ships broke through.

Ireland in the seventeenth century

The *Beibl Bach*, the 'Little Bible', published in 1630, soon became a bestseller. Very few seventeenth-century copies of this cheap little book have survived. People kept it in their pockets or in their homes, and read it until it fell to pieces.

James II landed in Ireland with a French army in 1689, to try to win back his throne. Irish Catholics welcomed him, but the English settlers, especially those in Ulster, feared for their lives. The people of Derry and Enniskillen declared for William, and Protestant refugees crowded into these walled cities. Derry survived a siege of 105 days, until English supply ships broke through at last and saved the starving city.

The siege of Derry gave William time to bring over a large, mostly Dutch, army. On 12 July 1690, at the Battle of the Boyne, William and his Dutch soldiers defeated James's French and Irish army. James returned hopelessly to France, and William's army took control of Ireland.

The Treaty of Limerick of 1691 gave Irish Catholics freedom of worship and safeguarded their land, but it proved to be a worthless scrap of paper. While William was occupied with his French war, the English Parliament and English settlers in Ireland ensured that Catholics were barred from public life, and lost more land. By 1714, Irish Catholics owned a mere seven per cent of all the land in Ireland.

The Presbyterian Scots in Ulster, like the Dissenters in England, were also resentful second-class citizens, in spite of their loyalty to William. The bitter divisions caused by the events of 1689–1691 have remained alive in Northern Ireland to this day.

King William's War (1689–1697) began a long power struggle between Britain and France, which later spread from Europe to Canada and India. During the War of Spanish Succession (1702–1713) Queen Anne made her brilliant general, John Churchill, the Duke of Marlborough. After his great victory at Blenheim in 1704, she gave him royal land in Oxfordshire where he built Blenheim Palace.

This tapestry still hangs there. It shows Marlborough's hard-won victory at Malplaquet in the Netherlands in 1709. The Duke called it 'a most murthering victory'; his losses were twice those of the French.

A united kingdom

In May 1689 William and Mary received the Scots crown and sceptre, delivered from Edinburgh. In spite of this impressive ceremony, they were barely in control of their northern kingdom.

In the Lowlands, the Presbyterian Kirk had been persecuted under Charles II and James II (James VII in Scotland). William had to promise more freedom for the Kirk, and more independence for the Scots Parliament. He needed the Lowlanders, for in the Highlands many clansmen were Jacobites, who set out to fight for James VII.

In spite of a Jacobite victory at Killiecrankie in July 1689, William's troops soon defeated the Highlanders. William offered pardon to the Highland chiefs in return for an oath of loyalty, to be sworn by 1 January 1692. Most swore the oath in time, but Macdonald of Glencoe left the journey until the last minute, and a blizzard made him six days late. A few weeks later, he and his clan were brutally massacred in Glencoe, while offering hospitality to government soldiers. Highlanders did not forget that William failed to punish those responsible for the killings.

Bad times in Scotland increased resentment against England. The failure of the Scots colony of Caledonia in Central America, partly caused by William's refusal to help, resulted in the death of 2000 Scots in fever-ridden swamps, and serious debts for many at home. Disastrous harvests, epidemics and trade losses through England's war with France all made the 1690s terrible years. In 1701 the English Parliament offered the crown to George of Hanover without consulting the Scots. The furious Scots Parliament threatened to choose their own ruler when Anne died, perhaps even James or his son, and abandon the war against France.

So, in 1707, when the English reluctantly offered good terms for a union with Scotland, the Scots reluctantly accepted, though many agreed with the Jacobite ballad 'We are bought and sold for English gold!' English gold paid off Scots debts. Scotland lost its Parliament, but had forty-five MPs and sixteen peers in the British Parliament. They kept their own law courts, their schools and their beloved Kirk. There was little enthusiasm for the deal, but it seemed better than any other solution. The four nations of Britain were now, rather unwillingly, one united kingdom.

CHAPTER 8
The wider world

❖

Two months after the terrible destruction of the Great Fire of London, Samuel Pepys wrote rather doubtfully in his diary,

> The design of building the City doth go on apace … it will be mighty handsome and to the satisfaction of people. But I pray God it come not out too late.

There was no shortage of good ideas for a new London. Charles II ordered that all new houses should be built of brick or stone rather than timber. Only five days after the fire, Christopher Wren, a brilliant mathematician and astronomer, produced a plan for rebuilding London as a beautiful city with wide streets and attractive open spaces. But people who had lost their houses and shops wanted to rebuild them in the same places. The old crowded street plan remained although, as the king had ordered, some main streets were widened. Christopher Wren still left his mark on London. He designed fifty-one new churches to replace the eighty-seven which were burnt and, soaring above them all, a new St Paul's Cathedral. Wren and his assistant, the scientist Robert Hooke,

London in 1753 by the Italian artist Canaletto. The new St Paul's Cathedral rises high above the steeples of Wren's churches and the new houses of stone and brick built after the Great Fire.

worked out the mathematical principles that ensured his buildings stood firm whatever their size or design. Wren had recently seen impressive buildings with domes in Paris. He decided that his new cathedral should have a huge dome, the first ever to be built in Britain.

St Paul's took thirty-five years to build, and cost £750,000. With foundations over 12 metres deep, and a dome 116 metres high, Wren's great cathedral has stood for over 200 years, surviving the second great fire of London – the air raids of the Second World War.

A coffee house opened in Oxford in 1651, and there were 500 in London by 1700. They were fashionable meeting places for men, where they could gossip and read the newspapers (which were now published regularly).

Brewers afraid of losing trade issued a pamphlet in 1678, said to be by the women of England. They apparently implored their menfolk not to 'trifle away their time, scald their chops and spend their money all for a little base, black, thick, nasty, bitter, stinking, nauseous Puddle Water'.

Wealth from trade

In 1600 England's wealth was still based on one main export, woollen cloth. By 1700, England had become the foremost trading nation in Europe. A great variety of goods poured into London and other ports. Merchants made fortunes importing tobacco, sugar, fine silks, dyes, spices and china, and then selling them in Britain and Europe.

For many people, living standards improved in the late seventeenth century. Pepys, a clerk in the Navy Office, gave a dinner for his friends in 1663 which, in 1500, only a nobleman would have served (with little difference in the menu):

I had for them, after oysters – at first course, a hash of rabbits and lamb, and a rare chine [joint] of beef; next, a great dish of roasted fowl, cost me about 30s, and a tart; and then fruit and cheese. My dinner was noble and enough.

Most of the ingredients of that London meal came from British farms and fisheries, but imported goods changed living standards more. Tobacco imports from the New World grew from about 25,000 kilos in 1600 to a vast 17 million kilos in 1700, and a pipeful of tobacco became much cheaper.

The new drink of coffee, from the Middle

A teapot dated 1670, probably the oldest in Britain. The Herbert family of Powis Castle in Wales received these instructions from London to make tea: add to a quart [a litre] of 'spring water just boiled and then taken off, ... a spoonful of tea and sweeten it to your palate with candy sugar ... let it lie half or quarter of an hour in the heat of the fire but not to boil.'

East, was popular from the 1650s. So were the new drinks chocolate and tea, sweetened with sugar from the Caribbean. Sugar imports rose steadily, and it became something most people could afford.

There was a high price to be paid in human suffering for this growing prosperity. Sugar and tobacco, the two most profitable imports, were crops which demanded hard labour in a hot climate. Since the mid-sixteenth century English, French and Portuguese traders had operated a terrible trade in human beings to provide this labour. English sea captains from London, Bristol and (by 1700) Liverpool exchanged cheap iron goods, textiles and guns on the west coast of Africa for slaves captured by local slave traders. Crammed into ships, chained to the lower decks in horrible conditions, these slaves were transported across the Atlantic to the Caribbean. Those who survived this hideous journey made a fat profit for the slave ship captains when they sold them to owners of sugar and tobacco plantations, mainly in Jamaica and Barbados. The ships filled up again, this time with sugar products and tobacco, and sailed back to Britain to sell their cargoes for yet more profit.

By 1700 Britain had a firm base in the New World. The old enemy, Spain, lost her grip on the Caribbean as the English took control of several islands, including Barbados in 1627 and Jamaica in 1655. On the east coast of mainland America the English already had twelve colonies; the thirteenth, Georgia, was founded in 1733. Fish and beaver fur were prizes further north. In Newfoundland and the cold wastes of northern Canada, French and English traders were fiercely competing to control these trades, at great cost to the native Americans and Inuits (called Indians and Eskimos by Europeans) who already made their living there.

English merchants had been trading in India since Elizabeth I set up the East India Company in 1600. They competed with Portuguese and Dutch traders for luxury silks, calico and fine muslin made from cotton, rare dyes, and saltpetre which was used to make gunpowder. Jahangir, the Mughal emperor who ruled most of northern India, granted English merchants a base at Surat on the east coast in 1615. Soon they set up more bases, with the guns and forts needed to defend them, and East India Company merchants and soldiers were firmly entrenched. Then the French arrived. They set up their East India Company in 1664. In the great sub-continent of India, as well as in North America, the stage was set for a European power struggle for riches and land.

Jahangir, the Mughal emperor, is receiving his son Parviz. He sits on a richly patterned carpet, in a courtyard of his palace. The Emperor's civilized and elegant court greatly impressed English visitors.

Fine houses and good fashion

The first original was a few fishermen's houses, and now is grown to a large fine town … the houses of brick and stone built high and even … there are abundance of persons you see very well dressed and of good fashion; the streets are fair and long, it's London in miniature.

This is what Celia Fiennes thought of Liverpool in 1698. She was a well-born lady who, unusually for an unmarried woman, travelled around England on her own (except for two servants) and wrote about her experiences. Glasgow impressed the writer and journalist Daniel Defoe in 1707: ''Tis the cleanest and beautifullest and best built city … here is the face of trade …'.

Trading ships in the port of Bristol in the early eighteenth century, bringing in, among other goods, large quantities of tobacco and sugar, as well as black slaves. In 1725 Daniel Defoe described Bristol as 'the greatest, the richest, and the best port in Great Britain, London only excepted.'

It was not only the rich who enjoyed the greater range of goods arriving in Britain. Travelling pedlars bought their wares in London and other ports, and then travelled great distances on foot, selling in villages and towns. Ann Clark, a pedlar from Donington, who died in 1692, left large quantities of cotton and linen textiles, as well as 166 metres of cheap lace. The textiles she and other pedlars sold were used in many homes. Some late seventeenth-century inventories (lists of people's goods made when they died) included a new luxury in small homes: curtains, to draw across the glass windows that had become common in Tudor times. By 1700 many villagers could afford more washable cotton clothing, and enough sheets to change their bedding more frequently.

Yet some people never saw any of this growing prosperity. They lived in hovels, where little had changed over two hundred years. In Scotland in 1679 (and also in many remote areas in England, Wales and Ireland) there were,

Such miserable huts as eye never beheld; men, women and children pig together in a poor mousehole of mud, heath and some such like matter; … when their house is dry enough to burn, it serves them for fuel, and they remove to another.

Winslow Hall in Buckinghamshire, which Christopher Wren may have designed for William Lowndes, a government minister, in 1700. This fine brick house is in the new style demanded by rich families, with separate drawing rooms, dining rooms and bedrooms, to give more privacy.

Strangers in Britain

*We pray you bring us 15 or 20 lusty young negroes of about 15 years of age,
bringing them home with you to London …There will be needed 30 pairs of
shackles and bolts for such of your negroes as are rebellious, and we pray you
to be very careful to keep them under, and let them have their food … that
they rise not against you, as they have done in other ships.*

Some 'strangers' (the old word for foreigners, used even for people
from a different village or town) had no choice about coming to Britain,
as this letter to a slave ship captain in 1651 shows. It became fashionable
for the rich to have black slaves, but we know little about their lives.

Very different strangers arrived in the south and west of England,
mostly in the 1680s. These were Huguenot (French Protestant) refugees
fleeing from persecution by the Catholic king
of France. English fears of James II's own
Catholic policies made people generous. In
London and the southern ports £40,000 was
collected to help the Huguenots. Some resented
the strangers. In 1693 the MP for Bristol
objected to the 'great noise and croaking of the
Froglanders' and demanded that they should
be 'kicked out of the kingdom.'

Most Huguenots, however, soon managed
to make a living in Britain. As they had been
forbidden in France to take professional jobs as
doctors and lawyers, many had become skilled
craftworkers, such as silkweavers, lacemakers,
clockmakers and silversmiths. They soon found
work in these luxury trades. Some became
successful bankers, doctors and scientists. Jean

*The Duchess of Portsmouth,
one of Charles II's mistresses,
and a great court lady,
wearing silks and fine muslin
from the East. She probably*
*bought her well-dressed
black serving maid like a
piece of furniture, from a
slave ship captain.*

*Death in a strange land, far
from home: a grave in
Henbury, Bristol, which tells
us much about the slave's
owner as about the young
African himself: 'Scipio
Africanus, negro servant to
ye right honourable Charles
William Earl of Suffolk and
Bredon, who died ye 21st
December, 1720 Aged 18
years.'*

After Oliver Cromwell allowed Jews officially to live and work in England, Jewish bankers, merchants and doctors formed an isolated community near the Tower of London. Their beautiful synagogue in Bevis Marks was completed by 1701.

A watch made by a Huguenot craftsman in London in 1702. Huguenot skills greatly improved the English clockmaking industry, and as most clockmakers in France had been Huguenots, the French industry declined.

Dollond, a silkweaver in Spitalfields in London, became interested in optics and spectacles, and set his son up in a business which has survived into the twenty-first century.

Diseases come and go

Disease remained a fearful spectre for everyone in Britain, young and old, although, after the epidemic of 1665, the terrible threat of the plague never came back to the new London, or the rest of Britain. It was dying out in western Europe too (but not in the rest of the world). It is not clear why this happened. As ships had so often brought plague with them, new quarantine laws, which stopped ships with sickness on board from entering British ports, probably helped.

In London, the rebuilding after the Great Fire prevented black rats, with their plague-carrying fleas, from making nests easily in the new brick and stone houses. The bolder brown rats, which did not carry plague (but were a health risk in other ways) probably drove them out. In other British towns too, fashionable new houses had the same effect.

Although plague disappeared, smallpox hit both rich and poor. In 1660 it killed Charles II's brother Henry and his sister Mary within three months of each other. Measles, 'camp-fever' (typhus) and many other infections were still killer diseases.

The high death-rate among mothers and babies remained. Queen Anne was more unlucky than most – she lost seventeen children, all except one as babies. There is little evidence that families became used to these tragic losses. An Essex clergyman, Ralph Josselin, and his wife lost two babies out of their ten children. In his diary on 21 February 1648, he tried to comfort himself as he wrote of his fourth child,

> This day my dear babe Ralph quietly fell asleep, and is at rest with the Lord … the Lord gave us time to bury it in our thoughts; we looked on it as a dying child three or four days. It died quietly, without shrieks or sobs or sad groans… It was the youngest and our affections not so wonted unto it. The Lord … learn me wisdom … This little boy of ten days old when he died was buried with tears and sorrow.

Although William Harvey had published his discovery of the circulation of the blood in 1628, the treatment of disease changed little. Doctors still bled and purged their unfortunate patients, whatever was wrong with them. When Pepys suffered from eyestrain in 1668, he confidently wrote: 'This morning I was let blood, and did bleed 14 ounces [about a half-litre], towards curing my eyes.' He was also lucky to survive an operation, still of course done without any anaesthetic, to remove a stone said to be as big as a tennis ball from his gall-bladder.

Attitudes and beliefs

After Isaac Newton and other scientists had discovered so much more of 'the great ocean of truth' (see page 90) the attitudes and beliefs of educated people were never quite the same again. Old superstitious ideas no longer made sense, as people began to look for scientific reasons to explain sudden illness, strange events or natural disasters.

This was especially true of the belief in witches, often unpopular and poor old women who were blamed for any disaster. Towards the end of the Civil War, Matthew Hopkins, a ruthless and ambitious man, was well paid for terrorizing East Anglia with a witch hunt. But a vicar in Huntingdonshire strongly disapproved, even as it was going on:

> Every old woman with a wrinkled face, a furrowed brow, a hairy lip, a gobber [projecting] tooth, a squint eye, a squeaking voice or a scolding tongue … and a dog or cat by her side, is not only suspected but pronounced for a witch.

There were no more witch crazes in England. In 1685, in Exeter, Alice Molland was the last person hanged for witchcraft in England. Lawyers, clergy and other educated people no longer believed in magic, although old fears and superstitions took much longer to die out among ordinary villagers. Attacks on 'witches' are recorded as late as the nineteenth century.

There were still many people in Britain, not all of them poor, who did not receive a proper education. Unlike the well-educated Tudor princesses, James II's daughters, Mary and Anne, were taught sewing, drawing, dancing and some French. Anne rather desperately tried to learn some history when she realized her ignorance just before she became queen.

There were more schools for girls in towns, but Basua Makin, a clever woman who had taught one of Charles I's daughters, wrote in 1673 that they did little more than teach gentlewomen 'to frisk and dance, to paint their faces, to curl their hair …'. Girls in her school in Tottenham High Cross learned languages, astronomy, geography, arithmetic and history, as well as the more lady-like subjects.

For most women a good marriage remained the only way to achieve security and a position in society. Unmarried women were poor relations. When Pepys took his sister Pall into his household, it was 'not as a sister in any respect, but as a servant – I do not let her sit down at the table with me.' He seemed surprised that she was 'proud and idle' and 'ill-natured'. He sent her home again, and as he thought she was 'full of freckles and not handsome in face', he was relieved when finally, aged twenty-seven, she found a dull but respectable husband.

This picture of Sir Richard Saltonstall and his family in about 1636 may show both his wives, in the same way that tombs often did. The pale woman in the bed is probably the dead mother of the two older children, and the richly dressed second wife holds her newborn son. The high death-rate, especially of mothers and babies, meant that marriages often did not last long, although divorce was rare.

'The Great Ocean of Truth'

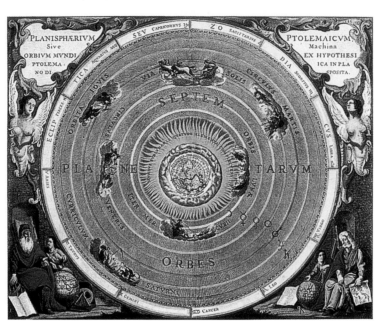

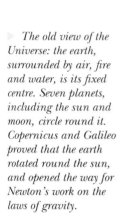

The old view of the Universe: the earth, surrounded by air, fire and water, is its fixed centre. Seven planets, including the sun and moon, circle round it. Copernicus and Galileo proved that the earth rotated round the sun, and opened the way for Newton's work on the laws of gravity.

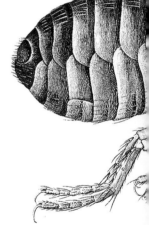

In England and Europe there was a great flowering of science in the seventeenth century. Mathematics and astronomy became especially important, as European explorers found their way in unknown seas using calculations based on the stars. Scientists studied the whole universe; biology, chemistry and physics were not separate subjects as they are today.

In 1645, in the middle of the Civil War, a group of English scientists met regularly at Gresham College, in London. They agreed not to talk about the war but 'discoursed of the Circulation of the Blood, the Valves in the Veins, ... the nature of the comets and new stars ... the improvement of telescopes ...' and other scientific subjects.

An illustration showing the valves in veins, from William Harvey's book

explaining the discovery of the circulation of the blood. It was published in 1628.

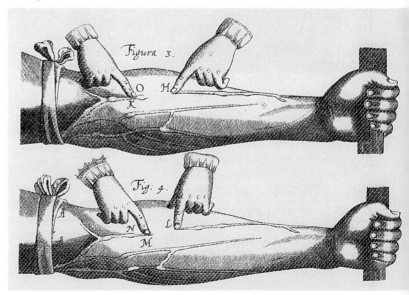

scientists still belong to it today. Charles II's interest made science very fashionable and amateurs like Samuel Pepys also became members of the Royal Society. In 1665, when Pepys was admitted, he saw Boyle's air pump,

> it is a most acceptable thing to hear their discourses and see their experiments; which was this day upon the nature of fire, and how it goes out in a place where the air is not free, and sooner out where the air is exhausted; which they showed by an engine.

Above all other scientists, the work of Isaac Newton on the laws of gravity laid the foundations of our modern understanding of the universe. Yet in spite of the fame he won, Newton thought little of his achievements,

> I do not know what I may appear to the world: but to myself I seem to have been only a boy playing on the seashore, and diverting myself in now and then finding a smoother pebble or prettier shell than ordinary, whilst the great ocean of truth lay all undiscovered before me.

Soon most of them were working in the more peaceful Oxford. They called themselves the Invisible College. The chemist, Robert Boyle, constructed his air pump there, helped by the ingenious Robert Hooke. When John Evelyn visited Oxford in 1654, he marvelled at the collection of scientific instruments he saw at Wadham College. Some of these 'magical curiosities' belonged to 'that prodigious young scholar Mr. Christopher Wren', who became Professor of Astronomy at Gresham College in 1657, aged twenty-five.

The Invisible College scientists helped to found the Royal Society of London for Improving Natural Knowledge, in 1660. Leading

The people of Britain

In 1709 Daniel Defoe described the population of England (and he could have included the rest of Britain) like this:

1 The great, who live profusely.
2 The rich, who live plentifully.
3 The middle sort, who live well.
4 The working trades, who labour hard but feel no want.
5 The country people, farmers etc., who fare indifferently [not very well].
6 The poor, that fare hard.
7 The miserable that really pinch and suffer want.

Sir Henry Tichborne and his family give out the 'Tichborne Dole', a gift of bread to the poor in the village, in 1670. The great house surrounds everyone, just as it dominates the life of the village. Sir Henry looks rather old-fashioned beside his visitors on his left, who are probably from London. The gentleman's wig, lace cravat and scarlet ribbons are in the latest style. Behind Sir Henry stands his large household, including a black servant holding one of the baskets of bread. The villagers on the right wait patiently for their 'dole'.

Society was still divided in much the same way as it had been in 1500, but by 1700 the wider world had changed life in many ways for the first four of these groups. Even those who 'fared indifferently' were better off than their parents and grandparents had been.

Yet there was little change for the poor and the miserable at the bottom of society. Richard Baxter, a Puritan minister from the west midlands, wrote of the poor he knew in 1691:

If their sow pig or their hens breed chickens, they cannot afford to eat them, but must sell them to make their rent ...The labour of these men is great and ... endless: insomuch that their bodies are almost in constant weariness and their minds in constant care or trouble.

If people living like this could have travelled 200 years back in time to the beginning of the Tudor age, they would have found the houses, food and work of the poorest very familiar.

THE ENGLISH ROYAL LINE OF SUCCESSION

❖

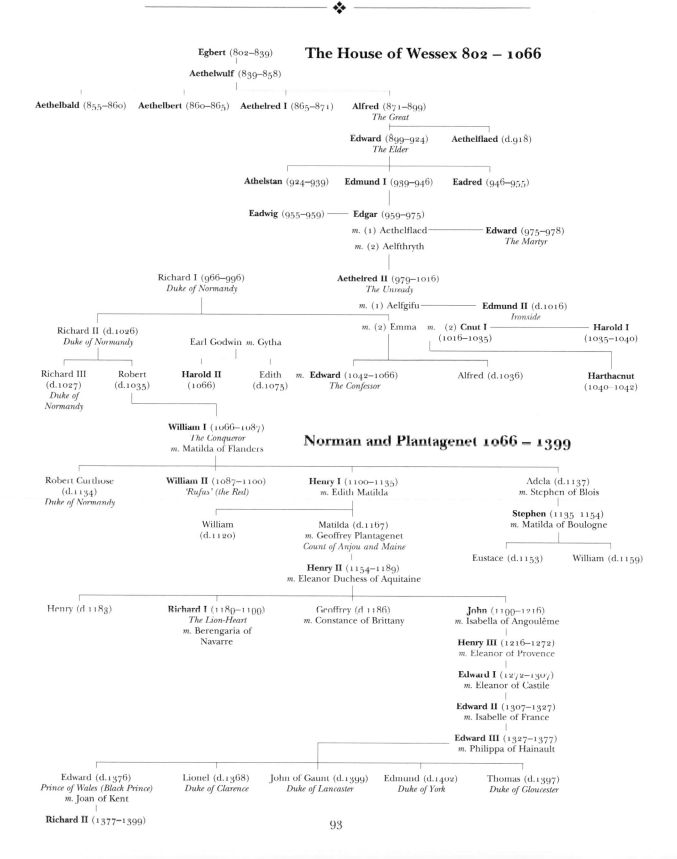

Egbert (802–839)

Aethelwulf (839–858)

The House of Wessex 802 – 1066

Aethelbald (855–860)   **Aethelbert** (860–865)   **Aethelred I** (865–871)   **Alfred** (871–899)
The Great

Edward (899–924)   **Aethelflaed** (d.918)
The Elder

Athelstan (924–939)   **Edmund I** (939–946)   **Eadred** (946–955)

Eadwig (955–959) —— **Edgar** (959–975)

m. (1) Aethelflaed —————— **Edward** (975–978)
The Martyr

m. (2) Aelfthryth

Richard I (966–996)   **Aethelred II** (979–1016)
Duke of Normandy   *The Unready*

m. (1) Aelfgifu —————— **Edmund II** (d.1016)
Ironside

m. (2) Emma   *m.* (2) **Cnut I** —————— **Harold I**
(1016–1035)   (1035–1040)

Richard II (d.1026)   Earl Godwin *m.* Gytha
Duke of Normandy

Richard III   Robert   **Harold II**   Edith   *m.* **Edward** (1042–1066)   Alfred (d.1036)   **Harthacnut**
(d.1027)   (d.1035)   (1066)   (d.1075)   *The Confessor*   (1040–1042)
Duke of Normandy

William I (1066–1087)
The Conqueror
m. Matilda of Flanders

Norman and Plantagenet 1066 – 1399

Robert Curthose   **William II** (1087–1100)   **Henry I** (1100–1135)   Adela (d.1137)
(d.1134)   *'Rufus' (the Red)*   *m.* Edith Matilda   *m.* Stephen of Blois
Duke of Normandy

William   Matilda (d.1167)   **Stephen** (1135–1154)
(d.1120)   *m.* Geoffrey Plantagenet   *m.* Matilda of Boulogne
Count of Anjou and Maine

Henry II (1154–1189)   Eustace (d.1153)   William (d.1159)
m. Eleanor Duchess of Aquitaine

Henry (d.1183)   **Richard I** (1189–1199)   Geoffrey (d.1186)   **John** (1199–1216)
The Lion-Heart   *m.* Constance of Brittany   *m.* Isabella of Angoulême
m. Berengaria of
Navarre   **Henry III** (1216–1272)
m. Eleanor of Provence

Edward I (1272–1307)
m. Eleanor of Castile

Edward II (1307–1327)
m. Isabelle of France

Edward III (1327–1377)
m. Philippa of Hainault

Edward (d.1376)   Lionel (d.1368)   John of Gaunt (d.1399)   Edmund (d.1402)   Thomas (d.1397)
Prince of Wales (Black Prince)   *Duke of Clarence*   *Duke of Lancaster*   *Duke of York*   *Duke of Gloucester*
m. Joan of Kent

Richard II (1377–1399)

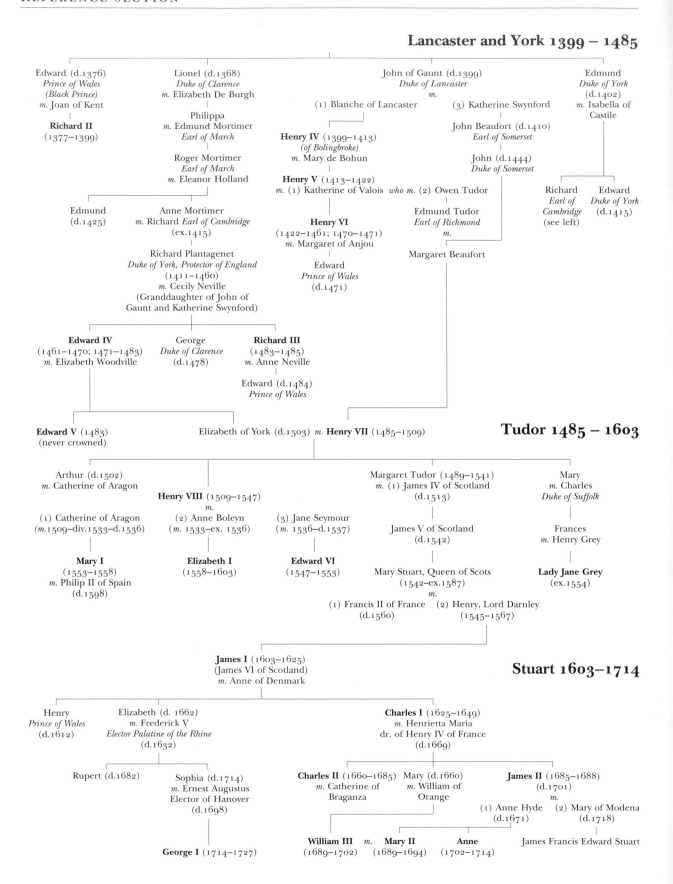

Lancaster and York 1399 – 1485

Edward (d.1376)
Prince of Wales
(Black Prince)
m. Joan of Kent

Richard II
(1377–1399)

Lionel (d.1368)
Duke of Clarence
m. Elizabeth De Burgh

Philippa
m. Edmund Mortimer
Earl of March

Roger Mortimer
Earl of March
m. Eleanor Holland

John of Gaunt (d.1399)
Duke of Lancaster
m.

(1) Blanche of Lancaster   (3) Katherine Swynford

Henry IV (1399–1413)
(of Bolingbroke)
m. Mary de Bohun

Henry V (1413–1422)
m. (1) Katherine of Valois   *who m.* (2) Owen Tudor

John Beaufort (d.1410)
Earl of Somerset

John (d.1444)
Duke of Somerset

Edmund
Duke of York
(d.1402)
m. Isabella of
Castile

Edmund
(d.1425)

Anne Mortimer
m. Richard *Earl of Cambridge*
(ex.1415)

Richard Plantagenet
Duke of York, Protector of England
(1411–1460)
m. Cecily Neville
(Granddaughter of John of
Gaunt and Katherine Swynford)

Henry VI
(1422–1461; 1470–1471)
m. Margaret of Anjou

Edward
Prince of Wales
(d.1471)

Edmund Tudor
Earl of Richmond
m.

Margaret Beaufort

Richard
*Earl of
Cambridge*
(see left)

Edward
Duke of York
(d.1415)

Edward IV
(1461–1470; 1471–1483)
m. Elizabeth Woodville

George
Duke of Clarence
(d.1478)

Richard III
(1483–1485)
m. Anne Neville

Edward (d.1484)
Prince of Wales

Edward V (1483)
(never crowned)

Elizabeth of York (d.1503) *m.* **Henry VII** (1485–1509)

Tudor 1485 – 1603

Arthur (d.1502)
m. Catherine of Aragon

Henry VIII (1509–1547)
m.

Margaret Tudor (1489–1541)
m. (1) James IV of Scotland
(d.1513)

Mary
m. Charles
Duke of Suffolk

(1) Catherine of Aragon
(*m.*1509–div.1533–d.1536)

(2) Anne Boleyn
(*m.* 1533–ex. 1536)

(3) Jane Seymour
(*m.* 1536–d.1537)

James V of Scotland
(d.1542)

Frances
m. Henry Grey

Mary I
(1553–1558)
m. Philip II of Spain
(d.1598)

Elizabeth I
(1558–1603)

Edward VI
(1547–1553)

Mary Stuart, Queen of Scots
(1542–ex.1587)
m.
(1) Francis II of France   (2) Henry, Lord Darnley
(d.1560)   (1545–1567)

Lady Jane Grey
(ex.1554)

Stuart 1603–1714

James I (1603–1625)
(James VI of Scotland)
m. Anne of Denmark

Henry
Prince of Wales
(d.1612)

Elizabeth (d. 1662)
m. Frederick V
Elector Palatine of the Rhine
(d.1632)

Charles I (1625–1649)
m. Henrietta Maria
dr. of Henry IV of France
(d.1669)

Rupert (d.1682)

Sophia (d.1714)
m. Ernest Augustus
Elector of Hanover
(d.1698)

Charles II (1660–1685)
m. Catherine of
Braganza

Mary (d.1660)
m. William of
Orange

James II (1685–1688)
(d.1701)
m.
(1) Anne Hyde   (2) Mary of Modena
(d.1671)   (d.1718)

James Francis Edward Stuart

George I (1714–1727)

William III   *m.*   **Mary II**   **Anne**
(1689–1702)   (1689–1694)   (1702–1714)

Hanoverian 1714 – 1901

Saxe-Coburg & Windsor from 1901

George I (1714–1727)
m. Sophia Dorothea of Brunswick-Zelle

George II (1727–1760)
m. Caroline of Brandenburg-Anspach

Frederick Prince of Wales (d.1751)
m. Augusta of Saxe-Gotha-Altenburg

George III (1760–1820)
m. Sophia Charlotte of Mecklenberg-Strelitz

Mary II (1689–1694)
m.
William III (1689–1702)
(son of Mary and William
of Orange)
(ruled alone from 1694)

Anne (1702–1714)
m
George of Denmark
(d.1708)

James Francis Edward
Stuart
(Old Pretender)
(d.1766)

Charles Edward
(Young Pretender)
(d.1788)

George IV
(Regent from 1811
King 1820–1830)
m. Caroline of
Brunswick-Wolfenbuttel

Charlotte (d.1817)

Frederick
Duke of York
(d.1827)

William IV (1830–1837)
Duke of Clarence
m.
Adelaide of
Saxe-Meiningen

Edward
Duke of Kent
(d.1820)
m. Victoria of Saxe-Coburg

Ernest Augustus
King of Hanover
(d.1851)

Adolphus
Duke of Cambridge
(d.1850)

Victoria (1837–1901)
m. Albert of Saxe-Coburg-Gotha
Created Prince Consort 1857 (d.1861)

Victoria (d.1901)
m. Frederick III
Emperor of Germany

Wilhelm II (d.1951)
The Kaiser

Edward VII (1901–1910)
m. Alexandra of Denmark

George V (1910–1936)
Duke of York
m. Mary of Teck

Alice (d.1878)
m. Louis IV of Hesse

Victoria (d.1950)
m. Louis of Battenberg

Alice of Battenberg (d.1969)
m. Prince Andrew of Greece

Alix of Hesse
m. Nicholas II of Russia
(both ex. 1918)

Edward VIII
Duke of Windsor (1936 Abdicated)
m. Wallis Simpson

George VI (1936–1952)
Duke of York
m. Lady Elizabeth Bowes-Lyon

Philip
(later Duke of Edinburgh)

Elizabeth II (1952–)
m. HRH Prince Philip
Duke of Edinburgh

Margaret
m. Antony Armstrong-Jones
1st Earl of Snowdon

Charles
Prince of Wales
m. Lady Diana Spencer
(d.1997)

William   Henry

Anne
Princess Royal
m.(1) Mark Phillips
m.(2) Timothy Laurence

Andrew
Duke of York
m. Sarah Ferguson

Edward
Earl of Wessex
m. Sophie Rhys-Jones

David
Viscount Linley
m. Serena Stanhope

Lady Sarah
Armstrong-Jones
m. Daniel Chatto

KINGS AND QUEENS OF SCOTLAND

MAC ALPINE
843–58	Kenneth I
858–62	Donald I
862–77	Constantine I
877–78	Aedh
878–89	Eocha
889–900	Donald II
900–43	Constantine II
943–54	Malcolm I
954–62	Indulf
962–66	Duff
966–71	Colin
971–95	Kenneth II
995–97	Constantine III
997–1005	Kenneth III
1005–34	Malcolm II
1034–40	Duncan I
1040–57	Macbeth
1058	Luiach

CANMORE
1057–93	Malcolm III
1093	Donald Bane
1094	Duncan II
1094–97	Donald Bane
1097–1107	Edgar
1107–24	Alexander I
1124–53	David I
1153–65	Malcolm IV
1165–1214	William I
1214–49	Alexander II
1249–86	Alexander III
1286–90	Margaret
1290–92	No king

BALLIOL
1292–96	John Balliol
1296–1306	No king

BRUCE
1306–29	Robert I
1329–71	David II

STUART
1371–90	Robert II
1390–1406	Robert III
1406–19	Regent Albany
1419–24	Regent Murdoch
1424–37	James I
1437–60	James II
1460–88	James III
1488–1513	James IV
1513–42	James V
1542–67	Mary
1567–1625	JamesVI

In 1603 James VI became King of England, Wales and Ireland. From 1603 onwards the rulers of Scotland are the same as the rulers of England and Wales.

PRIME MINISTERS 1721–2001

1721	Sir Robert Walpole
1741	Earl of Wilmington
1743	Henry Pelham
1754	Duke of Newcastle
1756	Duke of Devonshire
1757	Duke of Newcastle
1762	Earl of Bute
1763	George Grenville
1765	Marquess of Rockingham
1766	Earl of Chatham
1768	Duke of Grafton
1770	Lord North
1782	Marquess of Rockingham
1782	Earl of Shelburne
1783	Duke of Portland
1783	William Pitt
1801	Henry Addington
1804	William Pitt
1806	William Wyndham Grenville
1807	Duke of Portland
1809	Spencer Perceval
1812	Earl of Liverpool
1827	George Canning
1827	Viscount Goderich
1828	Duke of Wellington
1830	Earl Grey

1834	Viscount Melbourne
1834	Duke of Wellington
1834	Sir Robert Peel
1835	Viscount Melbourne
1841	Sir Robert Peel
1846	Lord John Russell
1852	Earl of Derby
1852	Earl of Aberdeen
1855	Viscount Palmerston
1858	Earl of Derby
1859	Viscount Palmerston
1865	Earl Russell
1866	Earl of Derby
1868	Benjamin Disraeli
1868	William Ewart Gladstone
1874	Benjamin Disraeli
1880	William Ewart Gladstone
1885	Marquess of Salisbury
1886	William Ewart Gladstone
1886	Marquess of Salisbury
1892	William Ewart Gladstone
1894	Earl of Rosebery
1895	Marquess of Salisbury
1902	Arthur James Balfour
1905	Sir Henry Campbell-Bannerman

1908	Herbert Henry Asquith
1916	David Lloyd George
1922	Andrew Bonar Law
1923	Stanley Baldwin
1924	James Ramsay MacDonald
1924	Stanley Baldwin
1929	James Ramsay MacDonald
1935	Stanley Baldwin
1937	Neville Chamberlain
1940	Winston Churchill
1945	Clement Attlee
1951	Winston Churchill
1955	Sir Anthony Eden
1957	Harold Macmillan
1963	Sir Alec Douglas-Home
1964	Harold Wilson
1970	Edward Heath
1974	Harold Wilson
1976	James Callaghan
1979	Margaret Thatcher
1990	John Major
1997	Tony Blair

INDEX

Bold page numbers refer to main entries; *italic* page numbers refer to picture captions.

ACKNOWLEDGEMENTS

❖

p5 Marquis of Salisbury, Hatfield House/Fotomas; p6 Nat. Maritime Museum; p8 Öffentliche Kunstsammlung Basel Kupferstich-kabinett, p9 College of Arms; p10 Nat. Gallery, London; p11t Museum of London, b Hulton-Getty Collection; p12l Mansell, pp12-13d Museum Plantin-Moretus, Antwerp; p13c,r Fotomas; p14t Nat. Trust, b Marquis of Bath, Longleat; p15 Nat. Trust; p16-17b Museum of London; p17t York Archaeological Trust; p18 Hulton; p19 NPG; p20-1b Royal Collection © HM The Queen; p21t Master & Fellows, Magdalene College, Cambridge; p22 Royal Collection © HM The Queen; p23 Robert Harding Picture Library; p24 NPG; p25b Ashmolean Museum, Oxford; p26t Nat. Library of Scotland; p26-7b Historic Scotland; p28 Mick Sharp; p29 b Mike Fear; p30 Thyssen-Bornemisza Collection/Bridgeman; p31tl, tr NPG, b BL (Ms.Eg.618,f57v); p32 NPG; p33t Mike Fear, b Hereford Cathedral; p34 Mansell Collection; p35 Baroness Herries; p36tc, cl Kunsthistorisches Museum, Vienna/Bridgeman, tr,b, & p37 NPG; p38 ET;

p39 Royal Collection © HM The Queen; p40 Victoria & Albert Museum, London; p41t NPG, b Michael Jenner; p42 Bibliothèque Nationale de France; p44bl V&A/Bridgeman; p45t ET; p46 private collection; pp47, 48t Fotomas Index, p48b Michael Jenner; p49 private collection; pp50, 51 V & A; p52 Popperfoto; p53 ET; p54t BL/Bridgeman, b Lambeth Palace Library, London/Bridgeman; p55 NPG; p57 Royal Collection © HM The Queen; p59t & b Fotomas; p60t NPG, b Courtauld Collection, London; p61 Fotomas; p62 Hulton; p63 NG; p64t NPG, b W & N/Nat. Army Museum; pp65, 66b NPG; pp66t, 67 Fotomas; p68 W & N/House of Lords; p69 Scottish NPG/Earl of Roseberry; p70 NPG; p71t BL/Bridgeman, b Fotomas; p72 Edwin Smith; p73l by courtesy of the National Portrait Gallery, London, r Magdalene College, Cambridge; p74-5t Museum of London/Bridgeman; p75bc NPG, br Private Collection/Bridgeman; p76tr Mansell, c Nat. Maritime Museum; p77 ET; p78 NPG; pp79, 80 Fotomas; p81t Mansell; p82 by kind

permission of His Grace the Duke of Marlborough, photo: Jeremy Whitaker; p83 Royal Collection © HM The Queen; p84c Michael Holford, b & p85 V & A; p86t City of Bristol Museum & Art Gallery/Bridgeman, b John Bethell/Bridgeman; p87l NPG, r John Blake/J Allen Cash; p88t Jewish Museum, London, b Museum of London; p89 Tate Gallery, London; p90t Science and Society, b Mansell; p90-1t Wellcome; p91t Michael Holford; p91cr Science Photo Library; p91br Portsmouth Estates/photo: Jeremy Whitaker; p92 Bridgeman;

All maps are by Hardlines, Charlbury, Oxfordshire.

Abbreviations:
BL = British Library; BM = British Museum; CCC = Corpus Christi College; EH = English Heritage; ET = E. T. Archive; IWM = Imperial War Museum; NG = National Gallery, London; NPG = National Portrait Gallery, London; V & A = Victoria & Albert Museum, London; W & N = Weidenfeld & Nicolson Archives